D1449140

The Refutation and Analysis of Falun Gong

《法輪功》破析

Written by Lao Cheng-wu

勞政武 著

iUniverse, Inc.

Bloomington

The Refutation and Analysis of Falun Gong

Copyright © 2012 by Lao Cheng-Wu

All rights reserved. No part of this book may be used or reproduced by any means, graphic, electronic, or mechanical, including photocopying, recording, taping or by any information storage retrieval system without the written permission of the publisher except in the case of brief quotations embodied in critical articles and reviews.

iUniverse books may be ordered through booksellers or by contacting:

iUniverse
1663 Liberty Drive
Bloomington, IN 47403
www.iuniverse.com
1-800-Authors (1-800-288-4677)

Because of the dynamic nature of the Internet, any web addresses or links contained in this book may have changed since publication and may no longer be valid. The views expressed in this work are solely those of the author and do not necessarily reflect the views of the publisher, and the publisher hereby disclaims any responsibility for them.

Any people depicted in stock imagery provided by Thinkstock are models, and such images are being used for illustrative purposes only.

Certain stock imagery © Thinkstock.

ISBN: 978-1-4759-3329-1 (sc)
ISBN: 978-1-4759-3330-7 (hc)
ISBN: 978-1-4759-3331-4 (e)

Library of Congress Control Number: 2012944220

Printed in the United States of America

iUniverse rev. date: 7/12/2012

Introduction:
The Intention and Methodology
of This Book

Falun Gong(法輪功) is also known as Falun Fofa(法輪佛法) or Falun Dafa(法輪大法). According to its initiator Li Hongzhi(李洪志), it began to be spread at the place Changchun, Northeast China in May 1992 at first.

In the 1980s, *qigong (chi kung*氣功) fever was prevalent among folks in the mainland of China, and many people practiced *qigong* to build up their bodies and cure diseases. Inevitably, people who taught *qigong* were a motley of good people and bad ones, among whom there were those who pretended to have "supernatural power", those who professed to have the ability to tell the past and the future of others, and even those who pretended to be able to communicate with "the other world" and absorb the fundamental energy of the universe…All such pretence has been intended for the pursuit of fames and interests; so, to a certain extent, they are more of a crowd of bilkers and swindlers. Those people's misbehaviors gradually raised doubts about "*qigong*" in the mainstay of society. It was in this background that Falun Gong came into being.

At the beginning, Falun Gong was viewed as one of various *qigong* factions, but before long, it began to become remarkable, and the fundamental reasons rest in the following two points: one was its public promotion slogan of "No Fees, No Presents, Voluntary Teaching of Gong"; such "propriety of means" showed its special appeal in the chaos of *qigong* fever, of course; the other was that it requires learners to practice mere five sets of simple actions which can easily show effects, which is much more practical than "the cultivation of *dan*" (pills of immortals煉丹) and "the cultivation of *qi*" (煉氣); because of its simple and easy entrance, people were able to easily persist in practice. Therefore, Falun Gong began to have many participants soon after it was spread. Li's true intention does not lie in these five sets of actions, however; actions are mere "Gong"(功), mere his artifice; only the so-called "Fa"(法) in his term is his purpose.

The so-called "Fa", also called "the Fofa at the highest level in the universe" in Li Hongzhi's term, is actually a set of "theory" which is a miscellany of concepts in Buddhism and Taoism, nouns in supernatural stories and some terms in science. This set of "theory" intends to establish a new religion with Li Hongzhi as its only "true god", and this set of "theory" is just Li's "teachings". Li constantly emphasizes that "I do not accept anyone who merely practice actions; the key point rests in the learning of Fa." The so-called "learning of Fa" merely requires people to accept his theory.

Therefore, the crux of Falun Gong lies in the part of "Fa" instead of "Gong". The problem is that it is not easy to thoroughly learn about his "Fa"; one has to comprehend Buddhist terms, Taoist terms, Western philosophical terms and the nouns of science to a certain extent, which are necessary knowledge basis common people can hardly obtain. So, many people of insights feel Falun Gong is improper, but they cannot easily point out how it is wrong.

In order to really and deeply acquaint himself with Falun Gong, the author made a thorough and practical survey in Taipei as early as in the summer of 2002, and then wrote the manuscript of this book. The author believes that this book is useful to those who intend to learn about Falun Gong, and is more useful to those who have participated in the practice of Falun Gong if they want to have a second thought on it. This book holds the basic attitude to research

Falun Gong objectively. We are well aware that "objectivity" has to be based on the following two principles:

One is the principle of facts.

One can never state a "fact" before he carefully surveys and verifies it. In other words, one should make remarks exactly on the ground of evidence, and he can never wag his tongue too freely. Especially, he can never distort or "trump up" any facts. So, this book has verified and given the sources of all its quotations from Li Hongzhi, and it has tried its best to give the sources of any other quotations in its demonstration.

The other is the principle of logic.

The principle of logic is not only the connatural law of thought of us human beings, but also the principle of existence of objective things; it is only because this law is available in the existence of objective things that they can be cognized by us human beings. Or from the point of view of Immanuel Kant's philosophy, which is at a higher or deeper level, the principle of logic is just the innate category of our minds, and only depending upon such a category can we know things in the world (the world of phenomena or the worldly truth). In this book, all discussion, research and judgment strictly follow the principle of logic; for if the other way round, all the discussion would turn out to be nonsense or sophistry, and that is what any books at a higher level should try to avoid.

To "accord with facts" and to "abide by logic" are the criteria to judge worldly truths. Therefore, we require ourselves to write this book by this criterion, and analyze Falun Gong in the same way. Hence, this book is precise in terms of its content; so to speak, it is a piece of relatively concise academic work. For the convenience of readers, however, this book does not take the serious form of common academic works; instead, it tries to meet the requirement of "explaining the profound in simple terms" in its selection and use of phrases; and in terms of the arrangement of chapters, it chooses an excursive pattern. In this way, readers may read it through in relaxation.

This book merely makes compendious refutation and analysis of some important issues about Falun Gong, expecting readers to have clear understanding of it. Therefore, the author has avoided abstruse and complicated discussion as possible as he can, presenting this book as a piece of mass reading material. In order to avoid the suspicion of superficiality, this book deals with some relatively abstruse questions in the form of "appended notes" where it is necessary. So it is advisable for readers to read pertinent notes if they want to make further research and acquire deeper understanding.

The research in this book merely takes Taiwan, especially the areas round Taipei, as its major sphere. But the five sets of exercising methods and related theories of Falun Gong are the same and do not differ because of different locality, so the author is convinced that this book is also suitable to the mainland, Hong Kong and overseas.

As it is mentioned above, the first manuscript of this book was written as early as in 2002, but after that, it was put aside and not intended to be published. But out of expectation, it is about to be published 8 years later. Why? Here is a long story, which should be told to the readers.

At first, the author lived in Hong Kong to study Buddhism for as long as ten years or so from 1994 to 2004, hence he had an opportunity to be a disciple of Master Nan Huaijin(南懷瑾), and thus luckily mixed with many virtuous celebrated people both from all over China and overseas, and he had personally learned many from them. At that time, one of Master Nan's disciples, whose family name was Li, provided a residence, which was called <Nan Yu> (南寓) and was exclusively for the reception of guests from all places and circles. <Nan Yu> was located in Kennedy Road directly up the Hong Kong Park, with its front facing northwards. Outside the house, one could have a bird's view of the Victoria Harbour, and see the Kowloon Peninsula in the distance. Inside the house it had a broad space and reasonably layout. It was a standard luxurious residence in Hong Kong. About five o'clock every afternoon, guests arrived in succession, and Master Nan usually came exactly at six to receive every guest; they were mostly disciples who have come to consult Master Nan, but the latter treated them all as guests and friends. Exactly half past seven, a dinner was served. During the one hour meal, the master encouraged everyone to express brilliant views or disclose new information, but he himself seldom took the floor. From half past eight to half past ten, fruits, teas and refreshment were catered after the meal, and it was a period particularly for everyone to ask for advice. During this two hours long period, most guests stayed, formally consulting the master about particular questions, or successively expressing their own opinions on political or social events both at home and abroad. It was always very lively. Occasionally, the master would give formal lectures pertinent to Confucianism, Buddhism and Taoism on the request of disciples; the lectures were recorded, which were kept as materials for the publication of books in future. Such pomp happened almost every day, so the master often described it in a joke as "*zhong-Nan-hai* and people's commune"; here the word "*zhong*" means "*zhongguoren*" (Chinese), "Nan" means "Nan's Residence", and "*hai*" means "*haiwai*" (overseas), while the "people's commune" means that people need not pay for their meals here. This situation lasted for ten years until Master Nan moved to Shanghai, and then Tai Hu Lakeside in 2004.

On April 25, 1999, Li Hongzhi mobilized ten thousand Falun Gong followers to besiege Zhongnanhai in Beijing, demonstrating through sit-down protest against the CPC Central Committee. This event was widely reported for days by the media in Hong Kong, so it naturally became a focus of discussion in the Nan Yu. During the conversation, we came to know that Li Hongzhi once begged through acquaintances days ago to have an interview with Master Nan, but in vain. I once asked face-to-face why Master Nan refused to receive Li. The master's reply was really wonderful, indeed, for he said, "That man has professed that he is superior to the Buddha. I myself am a Buddhist, how dare I venture to see him?" I was quite surprised at this remark, and thus had an impulse to find it out. At that time, I was teaching philosophy at the Hong Kong Buddhist College, and knew well the profound meaning of the fact that all the modern western philosophers unanimously revered

Confucius, the Buddha, Socrates and Jesus as four "paradigmatic individuals" of human culture; today, there is a man professing that he himself is superior to the Buddha. What was the matter on earth? Only a rustic bragger dared to say so, but Li was able to mobilize ten thousand people to encircle Zhongnanhai, so it is evident that he was not an ordinary boaster. So, it deserved research. At that time, my doctorial thesis was being published in Taiwan and the mainland (the version in Taiwan is named the *Fundamentality of Buddhist Precepts Studies* 戒律學原理, printed and published by the Lao Ku Culture Foundation Inc., and in the mainland it is called the *Buddhist Precepts Studies*佛教戒律學, printed and published by the Beijing Religious Culture Publishing House). So, many fellow disciples under Master Nan suggested in succession to me "why not criticize Li's mistakes from the point of view of the precepts studies of Buddhism". This matter is easy to say but hard to do, for the author could not begin his writing before he made a thorough and all-around research. Therefore, it was prolonged for more than two years, and the first manuscript was hardly finished by the end of 2002. Now the first manuscript was finished, and the wish to research Falun Gong was satisfied, the author had no intent plan to publish it; in addition, a publishing house in Hong Kong thought that the Beijing authority at that time was "shelving" the matter of Falun Gong, so the publication of such kinds of books may not bring in high economic profits, so the preliminary manuscript was put aside for eight years. If it were not my dear friend Lin Zhongjian (林中堅) who has done me a great favor this time, possibly this book could never be published.

Zhongjian is an old friend of mine for more than 30 years. He has served in the circle of culture over tens of years, once as the editor of several important newspapers and journals in Hong Kong, and a famous head of the China Observation Institute. In a word, he is an authoritative expert in the circle of today's political review in Hong Kong. Early this year, he paid a visit to Taiwan, and was informed of the matter of this manuscript, so he encouraged me to publish it soon. According to him, Falun Gong has been running both newspapers and journals these years, all its remarks evidently have intense political tendency, and it has constantly launched street movements. Step by step it has turned out to be a world-known group which is "engaged in politics under the banner of religion". So, it is necessary to publish this book at this time. The advice from an old friend as a political reviewer should be accepted, of course. That is how this book comes out.

At last, the author would like to explain why this book is named as "refutation and analysis". Now that Li Hongzhi has flaunted his "Fa" as Fofa (Buddhist Dharma), he should know that "refutation and analysis" is just one of the general characteristics of Buddhism. In fact, it is a Buddhist tradition to lay an emphasis on "refutation" and "establishment", and that is how it has developed a set of peerlessly profound theory. So to speak, the Buddha just established Buddhism by refuting and analyzing the wrong opinion of Brahmanism about inequality. Over 2,000 years, Buddhism has been constantly grown and developed in its refutation and analysis. For example, Buddhist logic (hetuvidya in Sanskrit) was just established to meet the requirement of "refutation" and "establishment". Especially, the Buddhist classics in the system of prajna are almost all about "the refutation of the incorrect and the promotion of the correct"; the most famous "three treatises" (the *Madhyamika-sastra*中論, the *Treatises of Twelve Aspects* 十二門論 and the *Sata-Sastra* [*The Hundred Verses*] 百論) all have the intention to refute and analyze the incorrect and thus present the correct. The *Madhyamika-sastra* written by Nagarjuna(龍樹) was just a book to refute and analyze all thoughts of "unchanging essence". Buddhism had the so-called "patterns and methods to refute heresies" during the period from its introduction into China to the theoretical maturation of all sects in the Sui (隋581--618) and Tang (唐618--907) dynasties, and those rituals were extremely sophisticated! Such methods and patterns to refute heresies can be divided into five types, but this book has no length to expatiate on them, and those who are interested in them can consult the original book about it <The 6th section in Vol. 1, *Introduction to the Treatise on Twelve Topics* by Fazang(法藏), 643--712] of the Tang Dynasty, see the *Tripitaka in Electronic Version*, NO 1826, T42, P0214a. And also, Mr. Tang Junyi（唐君毅） has

made an expatiation on it, see the Research on the Origin of the Tao道 in the *Research on the Origin of Chinese Philosophy*, p. 282 and infra, a third print by the Student Book Co., Ltd. in Taiwan in 2000>. In the light of the above mentioned, Mr. Li, the initiator of Falun Gong and his disciples should not think this book as an offense; instead, they should be pleased to reach the realm of dharma together with the author.

Of course, the expression "refutation and analysis" contained in the name of this book can also be viewed from the point of a common sense, and they do not involve any purposeful denouncement with a presupposed standpoint. Now that "Falun Fofa" may cause various confusion and delusion among the multitude, the author hopes this book can be useful for them to know the truth in analyzing its nature and related attributes. We know very well that any religious sects, no matter what qualities they have, certainly involve beliefs; and that in beliefs there are considerable irrational factors. So, it is not easy to judge and explain the content of any "religion". The author may be imprudent in many places, and especially, it is almost avoidable that he may be limited by his personal knowledge and understanding. So, the criticism from insightful people both at home and abroad will be appreciated.

First manuscript completed in Taipei on December 7, 2002
And finalized in Hong Kong in October 2010

Note:

1. Please refer to the Chinese version where this translation may raise any doubt.
2. Quotations from Li Hongzhi in this book are all from the Chinese versions of the *Zhuan Falun*(轉法輪) and some other writings by Li Hongzhi, published by the Taipei Yiqun Bookstore (台北益群書店), 2002.

Contents

The Content of Falun Gong

Falun Gong is composed of two parts: one is its "actions", and the other is its "theory". Now these two parts are recounted respectively as follows:

Actions

What Li Hongzhi himself calls "Gong" or "Gongfa"(功法) consists of mere five simple sets of actions. Among these five sets of actions, the 1st, 3rd and 4th sets are actually calisthenics which can only stretch four limbs, the 2nd set is "*zhanzhuang*"(站椿) (post standing), a basic kind of practice in traditional Chinese martial art, and the 5th set is the major part, which is in fact a kind of yoga practice mixed up with some "mudra" actions in Esoteric Buddhism. In essence, it is to sit still in meditation (a Buddhist style of sitting with a concentrated mind).

It takes about half an hour to finish all the 1st, 3rd and 4th sets of gymnastics in the light of prescription,① and the 2nd set of *zhanzhuang* also takes half an hour; the 5th set as sitting in mediation, however, needs one hour. In other words, it takes two hours to complete all the five sets as a whole. The true secret of Falun Gong just lies in here: If a person is able to constantly practice these five sets of actions, and exercise two hours every morning, his body will change soon, and spiritually he will have a feeling of relaxation and pleasure different from before. In fact, it is not that Falun Gong itself has any magical effect, but it is the result of persistent exercises every morning indeed.

As for physical exercises, there are two critical points in general: one is to choose a kind of exercising method suitable to one's own physical condition; the other is to persistently exercise that way every day. The first critical point is not hard to do, for if one is determined to choose, he surely can find a suitable pattern of exercise. What is really difficult is the second crux, for the inertia of human being is sheer; driven by such laziness, a person is always ready to find an excuse and thus give up his exercises half on the way; so, a person of "persistence" is seldom seen. Therefore, no matter what "practice" it is, for example, the fit-building exercises such as shadow boxing (T'ai chi ch'uan太極拳), Yuanji Dance,② Jiuru gymnastics, aerobics dance and jogging, any of them surely can bring benign changes both physically and spiritually after long (constantly over three months) so long as one exercises half an hour every morning, let alone that the participants in Falun Gong exercises as long as two hours every morning.

With a second thought of the five sets of actions of Falun Gong, one can find that the 2nd set, namely "*zhanzhuang*" (post standing), does not fit to aged people or those with cardiovascular diseases, including heart-diseases and high-blood pressure, and probably will cause dangers. In the exercises of this set of actions, an exerciser stands still with his knees slightly bent, which is commonly called "horse stance", and keeps this posture constantly for half an hour. It is very exhausting. Moreover, while standing, the exerciser stretches his arms upwards, besides above, forwards and downwards (called "*bao lun*" [embracing wheel]), each of these four poses needs to be kept for seven and a half minutes with concentration; doubtlessly it increases the pressure upon the heart, and can easily cause dangers. Actually, such "*zhanzhuang*" practice is a preparatory exercise for young people to practice martial art, and its purpose is to improve the stamina and the strength of stability of waist and feet. Li Hongzhi, however, takes it for the aged and the weak to practice (most participants of Falun Gong are women at or above middle ages), so it is quite wrong. Li says, "The persistent practice of Falun

Gong post standing helps exercisers have a sensuously smooth passing through their bodies, and it is a set of all-cultivating actions, which can improve exercisers' wisdom and physical strength, elevate their levels, and endow them with supernatural power" and so on.③ These are nothing but purposefully exaggerative remarks.

What really brings greater effects both physically and spiritually is the fifth set of practice of *jingzuo*(靜坐) (sitting in tranquility). The *chanzuo*(禪坐) (legs-crossing sitting in meditation) in Buddhism, also known as *jie jiafu zuo*(結跏趺坐), originated from the samana practice (monastic's legs-crossing sitting in meditation) in the ancient India; it is just the legs-crossing sitting posture of the Buddha images that we frequently see. In the ancient India, this kind of practice was common in all sects and schools; because it was both useful for mind and body, it was not merely Buddhism that adopted it. However, the Buddhist practice of its kind has more sophisticated and comprehensive pertinent theories and more natural postures, and thus has fewer defects if compared with others. Buddhism has its so-called "three kinds of learning", namely Disciplines (Sila戒), Meditative Concentration (Samadhi定), Wisdom (Prajna慧), which are the guidelines to learn Buddhism. Among these three guidelines, "meditative concentration" is the very kernel; without "meditative concentration", there would be no way to cling to "disciplines", and thus there would be no way leading to "wisdom", of course. Then, how to reach the realm of "meditative concentration"? Legs-crossing sitting in meditation is just a must practice.

As early as in the East Han Dynasty (東漢A. D. 25-220), Buddhist scriptures about meditative legs-crossing sitting have been introduced into China. Later on, Taoism also adopted such method of quiet sitting practice, only that the postures were slightly changed. It was Master Zhiyi(智顗) (538-597) of the Sui Dynasty (581-618) who improved the practice of meditative legs-crossing sitting to the profound theoretical level of philosophy about mind. Zhiyi was the initiator of the Tiantai School(天臺宗) of Buddhism, and his works on sustained concentration (dhyana) and stabilizing meditation (shamatha) and clear observation (vipashyana) are still the most authoritative even today.④ In the modern times, the most outstanding and the best known books about sustained concentration practice should be the *Yinshizi's Method of Quiet Sitting* (因是子静坐法) written by Jiang Weiqiao(蔣維喬) and the *Tao & Longevity: Mind-Body Transformation* (静坐修道與長生不老) written by Master Nan Huaijin. Jiang's work has been popular as early as 60 years ago, and Nan's work has been translated into several languages and sold well both at home and abroad. In addition, the author has also made comprehensive introduction about the various theories and methods about sustained concentration both in Mahayana and Hinayana Buddhism in the 3rd, 4th and 5th sections of the 6th chapter in his work the *Foxue Biecai* (*Selection of Buddhist Doctrines* 佛學別裁), those who are interested can find those books and exhaust them.

The fifth set of quiet sitting practice of "Falun Gongfa" is completely a copy of meditative legs-crossing sitting in Buddhism, and is thus helpful to mind and body to a certain extent. But it does not reach the depth of the practice of "stabilizing meditation (shamatha) and clear observation (vipashyana)", and can be viewed only as "the exercise of legs" of the preparatory practice of meditative sitting (a novice of legs-crossing sitting can easily have numb legs, and such phenomenon can be eliminated only after considerably long periods of practices), instead of any "cultivation of mind and nature" (Li Hongzhi often emphasizes that his practice method has been designed for the "cultivation of mind and nature"). It requires participants to sit still for an hour every day, in fact it is teaching people some strange "mudra", spending some time to divert the practitioners' attention at first, so it is not true Buddhist meditative sitting. Moreover, it does not pay attention to the physical conditions of individuals in sitting practice (for example, some people cannot sit straightly, some people have to sit on cushions, and so on), nor does it take care of atmospheres (for example, it is unsuitable to sit in wind outdoors, or otherwise participants can easily catch a cold, etc.) So, it can easily cause diseases if a participant practices as it teaches.

Theories

Li Hongzhi teaches people to practice the above-mentioned five sets of "Gong" (功), but what he really values is his "theory" instead of "Gong". He professes that the theory that he invents is "Fa" (法) or "Dafa" (大法), stressing from time to time that "The key point lies in the learning of Fa, and those who merely practice Gong cannot be viewed as my disciples".⑤ Judging from its content, the whole set of "Fa" he mentions is just a pile of Buddhist, Taoist and natural science terms frequently seen in newspapers, which are arranged in the light of his own "literal" understanding. He himself does not fully understand those terms for the most part, so he just draws a forced analogy by stringing unrelated things. Strictly speaking, therefore, his "Fa" cannot be called "theory", but some "nonsense". But do not undervalue such nonsense, anyhow. It is because of such nonsense that his poorly educated disciples have thus had a kind of religious belief, and made painstaking efforts to practice those five sets of dull "Gong" every day. Those who have improved their physical conditions through the practice of his "Gong" become more superstitious the other way round to the "Fa" in Li's term. That is where the true secret of his schemes rests.

In a word, nothing but "Fa" (theory) is the key point of "Falun Gong". And it is the availability of such "theory"⑥ that makes "Falun Gong" essentially different from such gymnastics or traditional Chinese style exercise methods (for examples, *qigong*, gymnastics, martial art and so on) as are purely for the purpose of fitness.

So, the main points in the following sections of this book are just the refutation and analysis of his "theory".

Notes:
1. For this set of practice methods, see details in a booklet titled *Falun Fofa Da Yuanman Fa.* (法輪佛法大圓满法)
2. A set of fitness-building freestanding exercise prevalent in the early morning parks in Taiwan and Hong Kong recent years. It is said to have originated from Taoism. Later on, it was renamed "Kang Fu Dance" (康福舞) in Taiwan.

3. See the promotion booklets compiled by the Falun Gong Research Society in Taiwan.

4. Zhiyi is also known as Zhizhe Dashi (Master Zhizhe智者大師), who had written four works on cessation and contemplation, namely the *Great calming and contemplation* (*Maha Shamatha Vipashyana*摩訶止觀), the *Exposition of the Development of Chan Paramita Practice* (*Exegesis of Dhyana-Paramita*釋禪波羅蜜次第法門), the *Six Wonderful Methods of Chan Practice* (六妙門) and *The Essentials of Buddhist Meditation* (also called the *Shamatha-Vipashyana for Beginners*小止觀). The latter two books are fit for novices.

5. See the *Zhuan Falun Interpretation* (轉法輪義解), pp. 167 & 184.

6. This book often employs the word "theory" to refer to Li Hongzhi's "Fa". The word "theory" is used merely in the sense of comparison with "practice" or "facts", and the usage itself does not suggest any approval or disapproval.

Li Hongzhi's Works

Actually, Li Hongzhi can hardly say he has any works, what convey his "Fa" is merely some writings compiled with several copies of speeches, and some video tapes and VCDs produced on the basis on such words.

Among his writings as such, the only thing that can be narrowly viewed as a piece of "works" is a booklet named "*Hong Yin*" (洪吟), which has collected 72 pieces of sentences. As the old saying goes, "*yin shi* (to recite poems吟詩), *tian ci* (to compose a poem to a given tune of *ci*填詞) and *dui duizi* (to supply the antithesis to a given phrase對對子)", now that it is called "*Hong Yin*", it naturally has the meaning of "poems written by Li Hongzhi". Opening that booklet, however, anyone with a bit common sense of poetry will find out that there is no piece that can be viewed as a poem, and possibly they can hardly reach the level of *dayoushi* (doggerels打油詩). So, what have been collected in this booklet can only be viewed as "sentences".

Then, what is a *dayoushi* (doggerel)? Folklore has it that there was a scholar named Zhang Dayou in the ancient times. Zhang Dayou was fond of writing poems, but all his poems were extremely rustic and vulgar, and cannot meet the standard of elegance. For example, he once wrote a poem titled "Snow", whose gist is as follows,

Snow（雪）
The whole river looks intact,　（江上一籠统）
There is a black hole on the well.　（井上黑窟窿）
A yellow dog is white now,　（黄狗身上白）
And a white dog looks swelling.　（白狗身上腫）

This poem is so rustic that it is really a joke. Because Zhang Dayou always composed such kinds of poems and amused people, the reputation of "*dayoushi*" was thus spread. Actually, it is not easy to compose a *dayou* poem, for although its words are rustic, it meets the requirement of rhyme and pattern of poems anyhow. Moreover, it seems delicate and charming the other way round sometimes when rustic slangs are included in such poems.

For example, somebody of the Qing Dynasty composed a *dayou* poem depicting the life of a husband and his co-wives, which is very interesting:

co-wives（齊人之福）
Not cold nor hot at the time when poplar filaments fly around,
　（不冷不熱楊花天）
It is the high time to sleep with his wife and concubine.
　（一妻一妾正好眠）
Three heads are laid on the same pillow romantically,
　（鸳鸯枕上三頭並）
Six arms hold each other under the same beautiful quilt.
　（翡翠衿中六臂連）
They look like a Chinese character "*pin*" when they opened their mouths to laugh,
　（開口笑時還似品）
And they look like a Chinese character "*chuan*" when they lie on their sides.
　（側身卧去恰成川）
Before he could hardly finish his job on the woman on the eastern side,
　（方才了却東邊事）
He receives a blow from the woman lying in the west.
　（又被西邊打一拳）

Another example was Mr. Liu Jianhua（劉建華）, a late senior whom the author had been acquainted with. As a native of Northeast China, he had been engaged in underground activities for the Republic of China during the resistant war against Japan, making extraordinary contributions by persuading the Prince Demchugdongrub of Inner Mongolia into turning against Japan, so he was a hero in the resistance against Japan. After he went to Taiwan, he served as a National Assembly delegate, and intently practiced Buddhism, becoming a disciple of Master Nan Huaijin. Liu was generous in his life, and was fond of writing *dayou* poems; his generosity was displayed in such poems. Once upon a time, he composed a *dayou* poem and presented it to Master Nan for instruction. Master Nan appreciates it very much, often mentioning this inspiring *dayou* poem to his guests.

Louses（虱子）
One should never shave off his hair, （為人切莫剃光頭）
Or otherwise louses would be distressed. （剃了光頭虱子愁）
Louses will hold their eggs crying, （虱子抱着蟣子哭）
And their eggs will hold louses wailing. （蟣子抱着虱嚎）
Don't be worried, the Heaven always leave a way out for living beings!
Slipping downwards, （別怕! 天無絕人之路）
There are still eyebrows to hold on. （往下一溜，還有眉毛遮住）

Here, the author wastes so much length just in order to say that it is not easy to even compose "*dayou* poems". Li Hongzhi will have to press on with his study if he wants to compose poems. If somebody has any doubt, let us pick up three best pieces which can be viewed as meaningful anyhow (it is another matter whether it is ok in terms of content) in the <*Hong Yin*> to appreciate:

The Enlightened （覺者）
(February 2, 1987)
The ordinary people do not know me, （常人不知我）
For I sit in the *xuan*; （我在玄中坐）
I am not in interest or desires, （利欲中無我）
There will be only me one hundred years later. （百年後獨我）

Li's Note: Written when I cultivated myself alone before I began to propagate Fa (dharma).

This is not poem at all, and its meaning is without rhyme or reason at all. What does the expression "sit in the *xuan*"? The word *"xuan"* （玄）came from the Laotze （老子）, whose original meaning is like this: The Tao is the thing-in-itself in the universe, but it employs the two contrary forms of "wu" (non-being無) and "yeou" (being有) to create the world and all things therein; that is called "xuan". So, "xuan" is a metaphysical descriptive term of how such contrary forms are able to create the world, and it is not a noun referring to any entity. A man's body and motions have to exist and stretch in certain time and space, for example, we can act in air, sit in bed, run on a road, and so forth, but how can a person "sit in the xuan"? If that expression should be understood as to "sit in the spiritual state of xuan", then, Li Hongzhi must provide some evidence to prove that he does have grasped the meaning and principle of "xuan". Or otherwise, he is merely talking nonsense by picking up a few Taoist terms.

Especially, the sentence that "There will be only me one hundred years later" is entirely against Buddhist thought, for the fundamental part of Buddhism is just the eliminating of "egocentrism" and the promoting of "non-self" and "emptiness of self"; however, Li expects to stand alone one hundred years later; is it not extremely ridiculous?

The Consummation of Fofa （佛法圓融）
(October 15, 1994)
Widely spread Dafa, （廣傳大法）
Save people out of Five Elements; （度人出五行）

Persistently practice, （恆心修煉）
Consummately surpass the three realms. （圓满超三界）

This is not a poem, of course; rather, it is like a pair of couplet, but the antithesis is very poor. And its meaning is especially unreasonable.

Li Hongzhi often professes that people who practice his "Gong" can "get out of Five Elements", etc., that is, the previous molecules and cells in human beings' bodies can be replaced with the high energy materials in the universe; he is completely talking nonsense! In the author's opinion, Five Elements (metal, wood, water, fire and earth 五行) are merely some marks that some Chinese people (for example, the sorcerers of the Han Dynasty, and those who are fond of physiognomy, *fengshui* 風水 and so on) use to stand for the mutual production and suppression of things, and their functions are just like such marks as A, B, C, X and Y in the modern Western algebra, or the four basic elements of earth, water, fire and wind （地、水、、火、風）in Buddhism; they themselves are mere symbols or code names. Li Hongzhi, however, professes that he can "get people out of Five Elements" and promiscuously borrows some science terms. It is really the "inferior superstitions" in Mr. Xu Fuguan's(徐復觀) term.③

Moreover, "three realms" （三界）are the "desire realm"（欲界）, "form realm"（色界） and "non-form realm"（無色界） in Buddhism; according to Buddhism, one enters the "non-form realm" when he reaches the highest point in his cultivation of sustained concentration practice. Furthermore, the "non-realm" is sub-divided into four levels: the Realm of Infinite Space（空無邊處）, the Realm of Infinite Consciousness（識無邊處）, the Realm of Nothing Whatsoever（無所有處）, and the Realm of Neither Cognition Nor Non-Cognition（非想非非想處）.④ Li Hongzhi professes to "widely spread Dafa" and teach people to "persistently practice", and thus the latter will be able to "consummately surpass the three realms", that is, to surpass the "Neither Cognition Nor Non-Cognition"! That fully indicates that he is entirely ignorant of Buddhism, and that is why he dare speak out such deceptive remarks.

A Visit to the Hometown （訪故里）
(September 11, 1997 in Yue Fei's Hometown)
Autumn rains are continuous as tears, （秋雨綿似淚）
I weep until my heart breaks. （涕涕酸心肺）
No acquaintances live in the hometown anymore, （鄉里無
故人）
The village has been ruined for several times. （家莊幾度
廢）
Eight hundred years have passed by, （來去八百秋）
Who knows whom I am? （誰知吾又誰）
I lower my head to mourn, （低頭幾柱香）
And present some incenses to the dead acquaintances. （烟向
故人飛）
Having fulfilled my wish of four forms of bodies, （四身心願
了）
Now I return to take people home. （再來度眾歸）

This passage looks like a poem in form at the first sight, but it is
incorrect in rhyme, tonal pattern and the number of sentences, and
the usage of words and the arrangement of sentence seem to be out
of the hand of a child. That does not matter after all if compared
with the extremely arrogance that it expresses.

What does it mean by saying "eight hundred years have passed
by, who knows whom I am"? Is he not obviously professing to be the
incarnation of Yue Fei（岳飛）?

What does it mean by the line that "having fulfilled my wish
of four forms of bodies, now I return to take people home"? By
saying so, he is viewing himself as the Buddha. According to some
Mahayana sutras, the Buddha had four bodies: 1. Reality-body (the
form of principles standing for the True-Thusness法身); 2. Reward
body (the body as a reward of Sakyamuni's numberless merits in his
numerous incarnations in the past報身); 3. Transformation-response
bodies (the body emerging on the occasion of certain events應身);
and 4. Transformation bodies (the bodies in the shapes of ordinary
human beings, dragons, ghosts and so on that the Buddha took for

fetching and saving sentient beings化身).⑤ Li Hongzhi professes to have these four forms of bodies, his arrogance is really ridiculous. From the primitive sutras of Buddhism, namely the four copies of *Agama Sutra*（阿含經）, we can know that the Buddha propagated Buddhism for more than 40 years in his life; although his numerous disciples revered their master very much, and even viewed him as a saint, they never worshiped him as a god with a "reality-body". The so-called "reality-body" and its development the "three forms of bodies" or "four forms of bodies" were the mere apotheosis of Mahayana about four hundred years later after the passing of the Buddha (see details in Section 9 titled Nonsense about Reality-bodies infra). However, Li Hongzhi, although merely in his forties or fifties, dares to apotheosize himself as such!

The above is the real information on Li Hongzhi's works. As for the written materials transcribed from speeches, there are more than 20 types circulating in Taiwan, some of which are appended with video tapes and VCDs.

Among these 20-plus recorded speeches, two copies are the most important: One is the *Zhuan Falun*, and the other is the **Falun Fofa Da Yuanman Fa**.

Zhuan Falun（轉法輪）

The entire book consists of 180,000 Chinese characters, and is divided into 9 units. That is the main material for Li Hongzhi to "propagate his Fa (dharma)". This book is matched with VCDs (or video tapes). The "9-day scriptures-reading classes" all over Taiwan just play the video tapes of this book for people. The video tapes are played for two hours every evening (one lecture), and are played 9 times that way (once a day). Its mere content is Li Hongzhi delivers lectures alone, and it is very dull and boring. He is just repeating something already written down.

That is the pattern of "*hong fa*"(弘法) (to propagate Fa) that Li Hongzhi has repeatedly stressed.

Falun Fofa Da Yuanman Fa（法輪佛法大圓満法）

This is an illustrated booklet about how to practice "Gong", i.e., it is the illustration of the five sets of "Falun Practice". In addition, there are also wall chart publications and video tapes (VCDs) with the same content. Both illustration and video tapes (VCDs) are all the images of Li Hongzhi, who alone performs various "practice methods".

In addition to the above-mentioned two kinds of most basic writings, there are also other three brochures, namely the *Falun Dafa Interpretation*（法輪大法義解）, the *Falun Fofa—Essentials for Further Advances* （法輪佛法---精進要旨）and the *Navigation* （導航）. These three kinds of booklets are largely the supplementary of the previous two, and contain no new content. Moreover, there are also the "teaching of Fa" in Australia and Singapore and some other places, which are also transcribed into booklets to sell publicly. These brochures are merely the repetition of the above-mentioned two basic illustrated booklets.

What is special is the *Falun Fofa—Essentials for Further Advances* (Vol. Two). This is a collection of words and writings after April 25, 1999; hence it mostly involves politics and encourages his disciples to engage an active struggle against the CPC.

In a word, Li Hongzhi can hardly profess that he has any important "works". Except one booklet that contains tens of pieces of senseless "*hong yin*", the other 20-plus ones are all records of repeated lectures and speeches. These writings as a whole all emphasize that Li Hongzhi is superior even to the Buddha and Laotze, and the level of their word usage can be depicted as "poor". It is such poor "writings" that Li Hongzhi calls "*jing*"(經) (scriptures)⑥ and "Dafa".

Notes:

1. The first chapter in the *Laotze*（老子） says, "Non-existence suggests the beginning of the Heaven and the Earth, and existence means the origination of all things...These come from the same source, and are all called cosmic mystery."

2. The Buddha had stressed the Three Seals of the Dharma（三法印） when he was alive, which says that "all action is impermanent（諸行無常）, all phenomenon is interdependent（諸法無我）, and nirvana is ultimate tranquility（涅槃寂静）". These three principles are like seals or stamps, which are the symbol of Buddhism, or the criterion to judge and discriminate "Buddhism" from "non-Buddhism" (including other schools of thoughts and heresies); they are very important, and Buddhist novices should understand this first of all. See the 8th section "Who Is Plagiarizing Fofa" below. See details in the author's *Modern Selection of Buddhist Doctrines*, pp. 43-44, published by the Lao Ku Culture Foundation Inc., Taiwan. Or the *Selection of Buddhist Doctrines* in simplified Chinese, pp. 14-15, printed and published by the Shanghai Ancient Books Press, July 2009, 1st print run.

3. According to Mr. Xu Fuguan, the Five Elements (metal, wood, water, fire and earth) usually mentioned by people are the five basic elements constitute all things in the world, and are similar to the so-called four basic elements (earth, water, fire and wind) in the Buddhism in India. The employment of the conception of Five Elements is mainly centered on the mutually generating and overcoming relations between them, so as to explain the changes of phenomena in politics, society, human life and nature. According to Xu's textual research, there was no such conception as "Five Elements" during the Spring and Autumn Period（春秋時代） and even during the early Warring States Period（戦國時代）, and that term never occurred in the teachings of Confucius or Mencius（孟子）. It was Zou Yan(鄒衍), a man

of the Warring States Period who mixed Five Elements and the concepts of Yin and Yang (陰陽), and then related Five Elements to politics. Afterwards, the concept of Five Elements further developed, and was enormously used in folklore divination such as physiognomy, fortune-telling and *fengshui*. Such evolution was a result from the inferior superstitions in the society. See details in Xu Fuguan's *History of human Nature Theory in China: Part of Pre-Qin* (中國人性論史---先秦篇), p. 509 and infra. Taiwan Commercial Press, 1999, 12th print run. As for Li Hongzhi's nonsense about Five Elements, see the *Zhuan Falun*, p. 83 and infra.

4. As for the question of "three realms", see details in the Li Hongzhi's Indiscretion, the 22nd section below.

5. For detail, see the entry "four forms of bodies" in the *Foguang Buddhist Dictionary*. Some Mahayana classics mention mere "three forms of bodies".

6. In accordance to the tradition in China, *"jing"* refers to the literature written by saints or that recording the words and actions of such saints, for example, the *Four Books* and the *Five Classics*. In Buddhism, except for that what Huineng(慧能), the sixth hierarch of the Chan School(禪宗) spoke about is called *"jing"* (*The Platform Sutra of the Sixth Hierarch*六祖壇經), any other literature that is named *"jing"* must be what were passed on by Sakyamuni himself. None of the other works can be called *"jing"*; instead, they are called "treatises" or "commentaries" and so forth. It is absurd that Li Hongzhi calls his lectures *"jing"*. It is not only due to ridiculous arrogance, but also because of the too low level of knowledge.

The Organizations of Falun Gong

Does Falun Gong have any organizations on earth? Many people argue that it has not only organizations, but also enormous and strong ones. But Li Hongzhi himself firmly denies it.
He says,

> "*The Falun Gong in China is merely a massive practice activity; it has no organization, let alone any political purpose.*
> *All people who participate in the practice of Falun Gong are members of the society…There are no various religious regulations that practitioners have to abide by, there are no temples or churches, and there are no religious rites. Practitioners can participate in and abandon it freely; there is no list of practitioners. How can it be called 'religion'?"* ①

Scrutinizing the pertinent writings and practical operation of Falun Gong, however, one can conclude that Li' s above remarks are false; this falsehood is not due to poor knowledge, rather, it is a sophistry. Why does the author say so?

What Is an Organization?
First, the basic concept of organization.
Human beings are social animals, so it is inevitable that they form various organizations. For examples, family is just a

kind of organization based on love and consanguinity; clansmen associations, alumni associations, countrymen associations and so forth are organizations formed on the basis of feelings; peasants association, fishermen associations and commercial chambers and so on are organizations based on common interest; political parties or political groups are organizations based on ideals and power relations; various academic groups are organizations based on the research of knowledge; and various religions are organizations based on the common beliefs in the ultimate pursuits in human lives. In a word, the human society is full of various organizations if in a broad sense, and no one can be separated from organizations. So, one does not have to taboo "organizations", and the point is what kind of organization it is.

Among all various organizations in the human society, two kinds of organizations are the most complicated and the most powerful: one is a political organization, for example, a state; the other is a religious organization, for example, the three most important worldwide religions (Christianity, Buddhism and Islam). A country dominates the people within its territory, and it has a very complicated structure. But compared with a religion, a country's power is not far-reaching or profound enough anyhow, for religion dominates man's mind, and man's mind has been the same since the beginning of man's history, so religion's power is both profound and far-reaching. And also, a "country" is merely an abstract collective noun,② while what dominates concrete and essential power is a government; but a "government" is composed of a group of people, and religion is often able to infiltrate the "minds of people" in the government, so religion is able to change a government at the end, the Rome Empire is just the best example of its kind.③ So, where religion conflicts with a state, although religion cannot evenly matched with the state in a short time, but it is hard to say in a long term. So, the civilized countries in the modern times (with respect to the history after the Renaissance in the 16th century in the Western Europe) had all gingerly dealt with the conflicts between religion and politics.

With a comprehensive survey of Li Hongzhi's all remarks and actions in reality, one can find that obviously he is intending to establish a new religion. This religious organization will have him as the only hierarch who is revered for all generations, the "Fa" (theory) that he lectures on as its teachings, and the "Gong" (actions) that he teaches as rites and cultivation methods. It is merely his mirage, of course, but it is a matter of another kind, and will be left to expatiate on in the following sections. Here the author wants to stress that he is really constructing a religious organization, and this is not libel at all.

Li Hongzhi's Organizational Operation

Second, let's have a look at some of his practical operations.

Li Hongzhi has established legal institutions called the Falun Dafa Research Society all over the world (in the areas where there are disciples). Li Hongzhi himself directs such institutions, directly takes charge of related affairs in each place. So, such institutions have played a role of "white gloves" for Li Hongzhi. Meanwhile, such "research societies" command local subsidiaries, and they are like Li's "incarnations" meantime. When Li propagandized his "Fa" in the mainland, Li had established a "Falun Dafa Research Society" in Beijing, and he himself took the position of director. Under the "Research Society", there were large stations (general stations for the instruction of Falun Gong) in each province, and there were middle-sized stations (instruction centers) and small-sized ones (exercise sites) under each large station. That was a three-level system. Moreover, Li had an absolute control over the whole system; the "backbones" or "instructors" at all levels were all members strictly selected by Li himself.

As for the operational pattern above mentioned, let's take a passage from Li's own lectures as evidence:

"In order to direct the practice, our Falun Gong Research Society makes unanimous decisions and directs everybody as a whole to practice when I am absent. All the decisions that the Research Society has made before are all with my approval; no matter where I am, they make decisions after they contact me by phone or fax. In addition, I have told them that it is a test for the

*Research Society. It is a test for the Research Society itself to see if they can lead everybody to do it well when I am absent. But I think it is ok, for the people who have stayed with me for long have been relatively familiar with my styles, with the things that I want to do, with the popularization of Fa (dharma), and with the things to do as a whole. So, I clearly point out here when I am absent, the decisions made by the Research Society should be abided by and carried out by all our instruction centers in each place of the country. As a tutor, he or she should be more obligated to abide by such decisions."*④

This passage has clearly articulated the functions and responsibilities of the "Research Society" and its close relations with Li Hongzhi.

*"But here is a rule: the director of each instruction center has to be a person who has attended the training class that I hold myself. The more he or she hears, the more profoundly he or she will understand; and those who have heard less often have less understanding, and even do not know what it is in some cases, so they could easily mislead other practitioners."*⑤

*"The directors of our instruction centers are all approved by our Research Society, and most of them are ordained or appointed by myself. This is immediately helpful for guaranteeing our Dafa's keeping its correct way."*⑥

Now that the qualifications and appointment procedures of "directors of instruction centers" are all directly or indirectly controlled by Li Hongzhi, how can he say it is not an "organization"?

The "Falun Gong" organizations in the Taiwan area have the same pattern in general. There was a legally registered "Falun Gong Research Society" at first; later, it was renamed the "Falun Dafa Institute", with Chang Qingsi(張清溪), a professor at the Department of Economics, Taiwan University, presiding over it.Chang's wife Chao Huiling(曹慧玲) is also an important backbone of "Falun Gong". Previously, Chao run a journal called the *Dashiji Zhoubao* (大世纪周報 weekly editions in Chinese language launched by the *Epoch Times*) in her name, which was distributed among practitioners for free. This journal had been designed for promoting "Falun Dafa", of course. Afterwards, it was developed into the *Dajiyuan Shibao* (大纪元時報 *The Epoch Times*), a daily newspaper, which is sold in retail shops all over Taiwan; its publisher is still Chao Huiling. Within the jurisdiction of the Research Society, there are 700 "exercise sites" or "9-day Fa-learning classes" all over Taiwan (a statistic in 2002). The establishment of these "sites" or "classes" has been controlled by the Research Society, of course.

Li Hongzhi argues that he has "no organization" on the one hand, but often professes that his "disciples amount more than one hundred million" on the other hand. It is really an exaggerated number, but such an exaggeration has to have its certain basis, does it not? If really without any organization, on what ground does he come out with the number of "more than one hundred million"? Especially, he was able to mobilize more than ten thousand disciples to encircle Zhongnanhai on April 25, 1999. It is impossible if he had no powerful organization.

In a word, Li's Falun Gong is absolutely an organization no matter from which point it is viewed, only that his organizational principle has an emphasis on the "formless" aspect (spirit), that is, taking Li Hongzhi himself and the "Fa" in his term as a sharp weapon to draw people to its side; as for other organizational forms (such as the procedures to register into the society, the lists of society members, the ID cards of membership and so on), all such things have been omitted. In general, such "formless organizations" that take beliefs as their essence are often much more powerful than formal political parties (for example, political parties in all places).

The Conditions for Organizational Success

Then, does it mean that Li Hongzhi's "formless organization" will achieve the final success in its confrontation with the CPC in the mainland? The answer is certainly negative; the reason is that Li's final success, that is, the realization of what is described in the above-quoted sentence "There will be only me one hundred years later" has to meet two conditions: 1. To comply with moral reason in essence; 2. To outmatch the CPC organization in means. Up to the present, no matter in which aspect, Li is still too far from meeting these two conditions. On what grounds do we make such an assertion? Let's demonstrate it briefly as follows.

1. It Does Not Comply with Moral Reason.

What is "moral reason"? The culture of man can be divided into many aspects such as family, economy, politics, sciences, arts, military affairs, law, sports, philosophy, religion and so forth, but overall, all these aspects are based on our spirits, that is, man's "spiritual self", "transcendent ego", "moral self" or "moral reason" in general. "Moral reason" is not only the basis of all such cultural activities, but also the dominator in them; everyone is consciously or unconsciously controlled by his innate "moral reason" to participate in and look on all cultural activities.⑦

"Moral reason" is even more distinct in religion. A religion that does not comply with "moral reason" at all is just a standard cult; on the contrary, a religion that completely tallies with "moral reason" should be viewed as an absolute orthodoxy. However, few can exactly accord with it. Usually, most religions partly comply with moral reason. The more a religion complies with moral reason, the more possibly a religion succeeds (the long-term continuance and prosperity of a religion); on the contrary, the less it complies with moral reason, the less possibly it succeeds.

Estimated in the light of the above-mentioned principle and standards, to what extent does Falun Gong comply with "moral reason"? I am afraid not much. This book is mainly to refute and analyze the essence of Falun Gong, and readers will have a reasonable judgment if they read this book through with patience.

2. It Is Impossible for Falun Gong to Organizationally Surpass the CPC

Can Li Hongzhi's "formless organization" withstand the CPC? In order to objectively answer for this question, we have to learn about a piece of history.

The CPC organization originated from Lenin's design; it is a kind of "fighting group with centered power", a mixture with Mao Zedong's "line of people's war" (taking the mass as a foundation, taking the mass as a vanguard, and taking the mass as backing). As history has proven, it has extremely strong battle effectiveness, and has almost really reached the realm that "There is no battle we cannot win and no fortress we cannot storm". In the confrontation between Kuomintang and the CPC in the mainland in the past, Kuomintang did not know its weakness and the CPC's strength, and had been always fought in a muddle, so it was completely defeated; after it retreated to Taiwan, it reconsidered the strengths of both sides, and made a pertinent self-criticism, finally finding out that its own organization was just too weak to stand the competition with the CPC. Then, it quickly developed two fundamental strategic guidelines respectively "against the enemy" and "for the internal":

(1) The principle against the enemy: It employs the 200 sea miles Taiwan Straits to sufficiently resist the CPC's invasion, adopting a long-term three-no policy (no contact, no negotiation and no compromise三不政策) to respond to the CPC's various attacks. Such so-called "three-no" policy is actually confessing that "I'm dreading you, and it is ok that we don't offend each other in future."

(2) The principle for the internal: It is divided into 6 strategies in general (organizational warfare, mass warfare, ideological warfare, psychological warfare, stratagem warfare and information warfare), which have been thoroughly researched and actively performed. The research was mainly made by the "Fu Hsing Kang College" (later renamed Political Warfare Cadres Academy政戰學校) headed by Chiang Ching-kuo (蔣經國), and the strategies were respectively implemented by institutional groups within their own jurisdiction, and were supervised by the "General Political Warfare Department".⑧

Over the 40 years (from 1949 when Kuomintang moved to Taiwan to 1988 when Chiang Ching-kuo passed away) during which Kuomintang and the CPC antagonized each other over the straits, Kuomintang had been frustrated although it had made all efforts wishing to organizationally surpass the CPC; not only it did not progress one single inch forwards in the mainland, but also it lost its power in Taiwan soon.⑨ This situation lasted until 20 years later when Ma Ying-jeou（馬英九）, a new leader of Kuomintang regained the power. Kuomintang then changed its mind; it does not expect to outmatch the CPC anymore, instead, it adopts a political line of "peace and cooperation" across the straits.

The above-mentioned is vivid historical lesson, which has been personally experienced by most people above the age of 50 years old; but does Li Hongzhi know it? Does he really know organizations? It would be too naive of him if he thinks his "formless organization" can really confront the CPC.

Notes:

1. See Li's essays respectively titled "A Brief Statement of Mine" and "A Few Opinions of Mine", in the *Essentials for Further Advances* (Vol. 2), pp. 4 & 14.

2. In the light of a general theory of politics, a country is composed of the four elements of territory, people, sovereignty and governments. What actually dominates the territory, rules the people and performs the sovereignty is a government, so most people often confuse a "country" with a "government". In fact, "country" and "government" are two different concepts, and should be distinguished; governments can be replaced at any time, but a country cannot unless it is annexed by other countries.

3. The ancient Rome Empire strictly prohibited Christianity at first, but later on, it could not manage it anymore, and even the emperors had been converted, so it had to announce Christianity as its "national religion".

4. The *Falun Dafa Interpretation*, p. 192.

5. Ibid, p. 145.
6. ibid, p. 147.
7. The theories about "moral reason" are very profound. For details, see Tang Junyi（唐君毅）, the *Cultural Consciousness and Moral Reason*, （文化意識與道德理性）printed and published by the Taiwan Student Book Co., Ltd., 2003, 2nd print run.
8. After Kuomintang's arrival in Taiwan, Mr. Teng Jie滕傑 （alias Junfu俊夫1904～2004) ranked first among those who were in charge of the research of "organizational warfare", and he was also the earliest initiator of "Society of the Practice of Three Principles of People" (also called "Reconstruction Society", popularly known as "Blue Shirts Society"). As for organizational warfare, see Teng Jie, the *Organizations and Stratagems*,（組織與策略）Taipei < Chinese Flag Monthly >, 1985, 1st edition. With respect to the Society of the Practice, see *The Establishment of Society of the Practice*（力行社的創立）, dictated by Teng Jie, edited and annotated by Lao Cheng-wu, published in the *Biographical Literature*（傳記文學）, issue 503, April 2004, Taipei. The mastermind at the General Political Warfare Department was Wang Sheng (王昇）（1917-2006).
9. After Chiang Ching-kuo passed away on January 13, 1988, Lee Teng-hui quickly seized power and kept it for as long as 12 years. Because Lee Teng-hui had intense thoughts and backgrounds of Taiwan independence, Kuomintang had actually lost its power during those 20 years. After 2000, Chen Shuibian came into power for 8 years, and Kuomintang was more of a party out of power. As for how Lee Teng-hui seized the power, see

the *Personal Witness of Kuomintang's Split in Taiwan*（國民黨在台分裂親歷記）, dictated by Teng Jie and edited and annotated by Lao Cheng-wu, in the *Biographical Literature*, Issue 502, 2004 (3).

Exaggerated Numbers of Practitioners

Li Hongzhi professes that he has more than a hundred million disciples; and his disciples in Taiwan also brag about this number. That is to say, there would be a Falun Gong practitioner every 13 people in the population of 1.3 billion in China. It is a frightening number. But is it possible?

We once made an on-site survey of the exercise situation in the Taiwan area. Taiwan is a place where Falun Gong most prospers, so a calculation based on samplings in this area should be objective and credible.

The period around 2002 should be a time when Falun Gong reached its summit. During those years, Falun Gong practitioners could be seen everywhere in the parks in Taiwan and Hong Kong every early morning, but they are seldom seen recently; obviously Falun Gong has been gradually left in the cold. Anyhow, we still calculate the number of its practitioners in the light of the data and on-site samplings in 2002.

The "exercise sites" in the Taiwan area, including 9-day Fa-learning classes and collective Fa-learning classes, amount up to 700 or so. In particular, the "9-day Fa-learning classes" and "collective Fa-learning classes" amount up to 200 or so, and the rest are true "exercise sites".①

9-day Fa-learning Classes

In principle, a "9-day Fa-learning class" is the congregation of a group of practitioners in an enthusiastic practitioner's house, collectively listening to Li Hongzhi who propagates his Fa alone through video tapes. Such activities last 9 consecutive days a month, and about two hours a day. What Li lectures on is not different from those in the booklet *"Zhuan Falun"*; actually, it is not different from reading the book through. The whole brochure consists 9 sections, and each section has the length of two hours or so. Li Hongzhi stresses that "the key point is the learning of Fa, so organize them to learn Fa."② Therefore, it is prescribed that each novice has to listen to these "9 lectures" first, so it is called "9-day Fa-learning class", and "9-day class" in short. The times to "learn Fa" each day are not fixed, and most happen in the leisure time after supper. As an on-site survey of several such classes shows, participants in each of such classes are not in large numbers, amounting merely five or six.

Fa-learning Classes

A "collective Fa-learning classes" is like a "reading party" in nature, and its activities are nothing but the collectively watching of video tapes (VCDs) that promote Falun Gong, the discussion on difficult questions, the share of individuals' "experience and gaining in learning Falun Gong" and so forth. It somewhat resembles the "Sunday sermon and testimony" of a Christianity church.③ Different from a "9-day class", such a "Fa-learning class" does not have 9 consecutive days lectures, and most participants are not beginners. Furthermore, its term is more casual, often merely once a week, two hours each time. Frequent attendants are not in large numbers, either; they are usually five or six acquaintances, and are mainly retired women.

Exercise Sites

In Taiwan, "exercise sites" are mostly located in parks of various sizes in cities and towns. Usually, they last from 5 o'clock to 7 o'clock in the morning, some from 7 to 9, and a few even from 8 to 10; the participants are mostly retired women anyhow, so we do not have to be so strict with their times.

Every early morning, parks all over Taiwan are crowded with all kinds of fit-building activities, such as Shadow boxing, Taijijian, jogging, Yuanji Dance and so on; except that some are accompanied with music, most are performed in silence; but mere Falun Gong is the showiest. They not only play Buddhist music, but put up striking yellow banners, with red large-sized characters saying "Falun Dafa (Falun Gong)". Under the banners are thick piles of propagandistic materials, which passers-by can take away and read at will. Despite such "wide publicity", those who really participate in the practice of Falun Gong are still in small numbers, and more often than not, there are mere three or four elder women at each exercise site. What they practice every day are just those five sets of actions (methods of practice).

Moreover, where there are the above-mentioned "9-day Fa-learning classes", "Fa-learning classes" and "exercise sites" simultaneously at the same place (a neighborhood consisting of several streets, for example), one can find out that those elder ladies repeatedly appear in these classes and sites. This is further evidence that the Falun Gong in Taiwan seems to be vigorous and in large scale on the surface, but its actual participants are not in large numbers.

The Calculation of Numbers of Participants

Let's reckon the number of participants at the very most: Suppose there are 700 "exercise sites" in Taiwan, each of them has ten participants, they total merely 7,000. Again, let's calculate it at the very most: Suppose there are 10,000 people practicing Falun Gong all over Taiwan, their proportion in the whole population of Taiwan (23,000,000) is still too small (again at the very most, suppose it is one part in two thousand). Compared with the numbers of participants of other freestanding exercises (such as Shadow boxing and Yuanji Dance, for example), it is absolutely much smaller.

Now, what result can we get if we reckon the situation in the mainland with the rate in Taiwan we have estimated at the very most (i.e., the one part in two thousand of the total population)? Suppose the population in the mainland is 1.3 billion, then the one part in two thousand is 650,000. In other words, even if we reckon it at the very most, still there cannot be more than 100 million Falun Gong practitioners in the mainland, and even there cannot be one percent of that number. So, Li Hongzhi's exaggeration is too incredible.

And also, we can have an estimate of it in accordance with the numbers that the research office of the Public Security Department in Beijing announced after the April 25 Incident. According to its statement, there were 28,000 "exercise sites" all over the mainland; if calculated at the rate in Taiwan, that is, each exercise sites is calculated as ten participants in average, the total number of participants is merely 280,000. Even if it is multiplied ten times, it is still less than three million. It is too far from one hundred million.

What should be stressed is that the above calculation is based on the rate in Taiwan, and is an estimate at the very most in the light of the data and on-site survey of Falun Gong during its summit. Judging from the exercise scenes in some parks in Hong Kong and Taiwan, we can see that fewer and fewer people are participating in Falun Gong.

The Consequences of Exaggeration

On June 2, 1999, newspapers and journals in Hong Kong and some other places published Li Hongzhi's large-sized advertisement "A Few Opinions of Mine"; on July 22 the same year, he published "A Brief Statement of Mine". In these two essays, he repeatedly professed that he had more than one hundred million "disciples" in the mainland; moreover, he even used such bragging and threatening language as follows:

*"Some news says that many people went to Zhongnanhai, and that some people thus became furious. Actually, it cannot be viewed as a large number at all. You can imagine it: there are more than one hundred million 'Falun Gong' practitioners, but only ten thousand went there. How can it be said to be a large number?"*④

A man who embraces the Tao should be modest, and should not brag the multitude of his "disciples". But Li Hongzhi does the contrary; moreover, he exaggerates the number of his disciples more than one hundred times, and easily boasts that "there are more Falun Gong practitioners than CPC members", intending to blackmail a regime. That will surely invite unexpected disasters. Li himself ducks out overseas for long, but challenges the CPC with his extreme arrogance. Is he not pushing his disciples in the mainland into great dangers? Is it the proper way of one who professes to cultivate "Truthfulness, Compassion and Forbearance" to achieve his own world reputation and status by pushing so many people into dangers? The *Laotze* says, "Violent and fierce people hardly die a natural death." (Chapter 42), Li professes that he has surpassed Laotze, the initiator of Taoism, but obviously he still has to make more efforts on the quintessence in the *Laotze*, and it is not that the simply scolding of others by frequently quoting that "When the lowest types hear of the Tao, they ridicule or laugh loudly--but if they did not laugh, it would be no Tao" (Chapter 41) would be a sufficient indicator of the attainment of "the Tao".⑤

To say the very least, even if "Falun Gong" practitioners amount as many as a hundred million, still it is impossible for them to resist such power as the CPC which has grown and thrived depending on struggles, for "Falun Gong" practitioners merely exercise for the sake of their physical health, once Li Hongzhi transfers their objective towards political struggles, those people would turn into a "rabble", and would be defeated and scattered if only they receive one single strike from the CPC. Therefore, Li's exaggeration of the number of his disciples and his attempt to threaten the CPC are really foolish carryings-on, which can cause only adverse effects.

Notes:

1. See the Schedule of Exercise Sites in Taiwan appended to the *Falun Dafa—A Compilation of Experience of Practice and Cultivation in the Taiwan Area*. This schedule is revised on August

1, 2002, and the book was compiled and printed by the Falun Dafa Institute in Taiwan.

2. The *Falun Dafa Interpretation*, p. 167.

3. An important rite of Christianity, and also one of its major propaganda activities. "Sermon" means that a priest or other professional personnel preach Jesus' teachings, and "Testimony" is that believers in the presence voluntarily speak to testify with their personal experiences that Jesus' teachings are really the truth.

4. A Few Opinions of Mine, see the *Essentials for Further Advances* (Vol. Two), p. 6.

5. These sentences in the 41st chapter the *Laotze* are frequently quoted by Li Hongzhi.

Li Hongzhi's Fundamental Deviation

Mencius said, "The evil of men is that they like to be teachers of others." (Li Lou [part one] 孟子 •　離婁上). Why to like to be teachers of others? In the light of the Consciousness-only Theory in Buddhism, it is the consequence of "self-pride", a bad kind of mentality. That should be where Li's fundamental deviation in his character rests. As for this point, possibly he himself is not aware, let alone those who are deluded by him and thus choose to practice Falun Gong.

Li Hongzhi has reached a seldom seen extent in terms of liking to "be teachers of others". In all his lectures, writings, video records and booklets, he has not only put up an obvious air of a "master", but brazenly professed to be a "master", and directly called practitioners "disciples". Such an impolite form of address sounds so shamelessly boastful that it is disgusting.

The Relations between Master and Disciples

Anyone of a bit cultural cultivation would be aware that a true master would never profess to be a "master", for once he did so, he would be no master anymore. A vivid example is just Master Nan Huaijin. Nan is a recognized contemporary master of the studies of the Chan School, and many people in the mainland call him a "master of traditional Chinese learning", but he himself disrelishes very much being called a "master" or a "living Buddha". He often warns his juniors beside him half jokingly as such, "Be sure not to think yourselves 'outstanding', or you're getting 'out of it'!" He is even reluctant to admit him as a "teacher"; for tens of years, no matter whether in Taiwan, the USA or Hong Kong, there have been numberless people who heartedly want to respect him as a master, but he himself repeatedly states that except the students whom he taught when he was a teacher in universities, he denies that any other people are his disciples. With regards to the juniors who have come to see him, he treats them all as friends, and he never poses as a "teacher". Some young people greeted him with *kowtow* (叩頭) when they saw him, which is the most solemn etiquette coming down from the ancient times, he immediately returned their greetings the same way; embarrassed then and there, they dare not make such formal salute to him anymore. Master Nan has a worldwide reputation because he deserves it,① and it is absolute not that he flukes it through arrogance and poses.

It is an outstanding aspect of traditional Chinese culture to "respect a teacher and value the Tao" (尊師重道), and it is very important. But the so-called respect to a teacher should be the sincere respect that others heartedly show to you, and it is not that you pose to require others' respect. Even if the others really regard you as a master, you shall not breach etiquettes or rites by addressing yourself as a master. Since the very ancient times, the Chinese people have defined the relations between master and disciples half as those between teacher and students and half as between friends; that is what is meant by the expression "*yi shi yi you*" (亦師亦友half a master and half a friend), and the respect between master and disciples is mutual. So, when a master wrote to his disciples, he never called himself "master"; instead, he should refer to himself as "I the unwise" to show his modesty. As for the address to disciples in the ancient times, some masters called them "gentlemen" (In Japan, students are still addressed this way even up to now), and they called the latter "*xue di*" (學弟younger brother as a fellow scholar) or "*xian di*" (賢棣virtuous younger brother) at the least. Even in today's formal schools in the mainland and Taiwan, teachers still address students with respect as "*tongxue*" (同學people who learn together). Li Hongzhi, however, calls himself "master" and others "disciples" in his lectures and writings. Such a rude man he is! It is almost unbelievable.

The Chinese nation has been proud of its reputation as a "nation of etiquette and righteousnes" (禮義之邦). Politeness is absolutely not unimportant superficial conduct; it is the "lubricant" between people, and also the cause of blessings and mishaps. A person's etiquette is a reliable indicator of the depth of his personal cultivation. A man who knows nothing about basic politeness has the imprudence to profess to be a "master" and brazenly call others "disciples"; the only impression that he leaves with people can be mere rudeness.

Extreme Arrogance

Li Hongzhi's demerits are not limited to his lack of politeness and etiquette; his arrogance shown through the "Fa" that he promotes is especially breathtaking. For example:

--He asserts that Laotze's Taoism merely promotes "truthfulness", the Buddha's Buddhism merely promotes "Compassion". In Li's eyes, these are one-sided teachings, and thus are not superior enough. But his "Dafa" promotes "Truthfulness, Compassion and Forbearance", and is the consummate Dafa at the highest level in the universe. Ever since the remotest times, he has been the only one who spreads such "Dafa"; and there will not be another one who does so until the indefinite future. So, the contemporary people are really so lucky that they happen to live in the "true dharma" period when he stays in this world.

--He professes that he has numerous "reality-bodies". So long as people listen to his lectures and/or read his books, his "reality-bodies" will imbed a "Falun" in their *dantian* (丹田a central point at the lower belly). That event hence, it does not matter even if you do "not practice Gong", because that "Falun" will automatically "exercise" you, improve your realm, and help you attain true achievements.

--He brazenly calls his writings "*jing*" (scriptures). No disciples are allowed to explain or explicate his "scriptures". The reason is that he is the only "master", and no one can be a master at present, nor in the future. Hence, Li Hongzhi is a master both unprecedented and peerless in the future, and he is the only one deserving reverence.

The above are three examples that the author randomly picks up from Li's writings. In fact, all his "works" are full of such arrogant words, which are both amazing and ridiculous.

Mature ears naturally bend stalks down, and a man of true cultivation will never be arrogant. People of arrogance may see their better days for a moment by chance, but they will have bad ends after all. The best evidence is that all the virtuous people in the ancient times advocated modesty.

The Modesty and Self-restraint of Taoism

The kernel spirit of Taoism is modesty and self-restraint. The *Laotze* has mere five thousand Chinese characters, but many chapters stress that a person should be modest and self-abased. In fact, it is the major idea of the whole set of Taoist thoughts. Now let's quote a few chapters from it:

> *"I have three treasures to be maintained and cherished: the first is love; the second is frugality; the third is not pushing oneself ahead of others." (Chapter 67)*

Here, the expression "not pushing oneself ahead of others" just means modesty and self-abasement. Modesty and self-restraint are very beneficial:

> *"He does not show himself much, he is therefore luminous and clear. He does not define himself, therefore he is distinct. He does not boast, therefore people give him credit: he succeeds by that. He's never outright proud of his work, and therefore he endures." (Chapter 24)*

This chapter means that a person's achievements will appear more remarkable if he does not like to show himself off; that a person's merits will be conspicuous if he is not self-righteous; and that a person's everything will last for long if he does not think highly of himself. Then what will it be if he breaches such self-abasement?

> *"He who does his own looking sees little, and he who shows or reveals himself is hardly luminous. He who justifies and defines himself isn't subsequently distinct. He who boasts of what he will do succeeds in nothing; he who brags does not endure for long, he who is proud of his work, achieves nothing well lasting."* (Chapter 24)

A person who likes to show himself off is disgusting, so his achievements will be neglected instead; a self-righteous person will be loathed so that others will not notice his merits, so his achievements will be denied even if he has some; and that conceit will retrain a person's mind, so nothing can last long.

> *"They give them life, but do not take possession of them. They act, but do not rely on their own ability. They accomplish, but claim no credit. Because they claim no credit, their accomplishment remains with them."* (Chapter 2)

This passage means that a saint's conduct meets the standard of the Heavenly Tao. The Heaven and the Earth beget all things in the world, but they do not try to possess the latter as their own; the Heaven and the Earth foster all things in the world, but they do not brag their capability; the Heaven and the Earth consummate all things in the world, but they do not show off their contribution. Just because they do not think highly of themselves, their credits last for long instead.

> *"The destination of all things, yet claiming nothing, it may be considered great. Because it never claims greatness, its greatness is achieved."* (Chapter 34)

This passage has a similar meaning with the sentence "Because they claim no credit, their accomplishment remains with them" in the quotation supra; actually it is just the "dialectical view" that today's politicians frequently talk about.

Li Hongzhi, who is fond of quoting a few from the *Laotze*, is obviously unfamiliar with the above-mentioned instruction by the great sage, let alone putting it into practice, that is why he brags that he has "a hundred million" disciples. He would be really great if he really had a hundred million disciples and if he had not boasted himself all the time. Contrarily, he has made himself a joke by exaggerating the number of his disciples, like a frog which swells its belly to threaten rivals.

The Buddha Strictly Prohibited Groundless Remarks

Sakyamuni was a very modest saint. He was very polite to his disciples when he lived with them in his life (The Buddha habitually called others "Great Bodhisattva", "good man", "good woman" and so on). According to the *Agama Sutra* and some other reliable scriptures, he had stressed that he was "also a member of sangha"—With this expression, he expressed that he was not a sacred master superior to anyone else, and that he was merely a member of monastic groups. Later on, Sakyamuni was respected as "the master of Heavenly Gods and human beings", "sadhu", "God" and "the Buddha", but these honorific titles were given to him in Mahayana sutras after his passing, especially five hundred years later after his passing, and it is absolutely not that he called himself when he lived. Did he ever resemble Li Hongzhi, who is merely in his forties but calls many a grandma and a grandpa "disciples" face to face although the latter are actually his seniors? Is it not absurd? If he had really known a little bit Buddhism, he would not have been so arrogant.

In the Consciousness-only Theory of Buddhism, arrogance is called "mang" (慢self-conceit); it is one of "serious defilements", and a fundamental cause of troubles that should be immediately eliminated.② Once a Buddhist professes to have extremely high achievements as Li has done, he will be viewed as has breached the principal rule of "serious groundless remarks", and will receive the serious punishment of being expelled from sangha. Here, it involves an important rule of Buddhism, which should be briefly introduced on this occasion.

The precepts of Buddhism were all established by the Buddha; because they were "established on the occasion of commitment of wrongdoings" (when somebody did something wrong, the Buddha established a rule), precepts became very complicated after more than 40 years' accumulation. For example, there are as many as 250 precepts for male monastic Buddhists, and 348 for female ones. In addition, there are such items as "five precepts", "eight precepts", "ten precepts" and "Bodhisattva precepts". Nevertheless, what are most fundamental are the "five precepts", and other precepts are all derivatives from these five precepts. The so-called "five precepts" （五戒）are "no killing, no improper sex, no steal, no groundless remarks, and no drinking of alcohol".③ In particular, the fourth precept about "groundless remarks" (妄言) is just directed against a man like Li Hongzhi, who professes to have the highest cultivation but in fact knows the least politeness, and is even unable to be an ordinary person. A Buddhist monastic would be expelled from Sangha forever once he breaches such an important precept.

Confucianism Stresses Modesty

The Confucianism in China also advocates modesty. In the *Book of Changes* (易經), there is a diagram named "*qian*" (謙卦), which is specially designed for modesty, and has discussed this issue most thoroughly:

> *"It is the law of heaven to make fullness empty and to make full what is modest, it is the law of earth to alter the full and to contribute to the modest, it is the law of fate to undermine what is full and to prosper the modest, and men also hate fullness and love the modest. When a man holds a high position and is nevertheless modest, he shines with the light of wisdom; if he is in a lowly position and is modest, he cannot be passed by. Thus the superior man can carry out his work to the end without boasting of what he has achieved." (Annotation to the Diagram Qian [Modesty])*

This passage in the *Book of Changes* is very explicit: An arrogant man is not a gentleman but a base person, and he will certainly have a bad end.

Take Confucius as another example, who has been revered as a "master and example of numerous generations" by later generations, and ranks among the four world "great philosophers" recognized in the modern times. ④ He had never thought of himself as a "saint" in his life. Some people praised Confucius as had attained the consummate personality of "sainthood and benevolence", but Confucius said, "Could I venture to call myself a sage or a benevolent man? At most, it might be said that I so pursue without losing interest and instruct others relentlessly." (Shuer in *The Analects of Confucius* 論語・述而) So modest a truly saint was! Similar remarks can be found in the *Writings of Mencius*, too:

> *"A Sage is what I cannot rise to. I learn without satiety, and teach without being tired." (Gongsun Chou [part two]* 孟子・公孫丑上 *)*

"To learn without satiety, and teach without being tired," that is just the attitude a true master is supposed to have.

Anti-intellectualism

Li Hongzhi, who is fond of posing to be a "master", admits that he has only the educational ground of high school,⑤ and that he did not go to college. Why did he not go to college? He surprisingly explained as such:

> *"The very reason why I did not go to college after I graduated from a high school is that I cannot form various concepts, theorems, definitions, laws, theories or various regulated things. In lecturing on the Fa (dharma), the cosmic law cannot be mixed with such artificial things at all, cannot be intervened by the ideas of human beings at all."⑥*

This passage deserves in-depth research. Was he unable to be matriculated or did he not go to college after he was admitted to a college on earth? That involves Li Hongzhi's fundamental character, and thus makes difference. If it is in the former case, the truth would be that he was unable to be matriculated at all, and that his remarks are mere concealment showing his "acid grapes" mentality, and a kind of cunning and hypocritical excuse. If it is in the latter case, that is, he chose not to go to college although he had been matriculated, then he can be viewed as a man of remarkable character and aspiration. But the question is, for the sake of public creditability, he has to present evidence (the admission notice from the university, for example).

In fact, even if what Li says is true, that is, he had really been matriculated but he himself had chosen not to go to college, this quotation of his remarks is still absurd. He says he wants to abandon all things involving human activities, then what is "Li Hongzhi"? Is it not a name given and used by human beings? He should have abandoned this name too if his remarks make any sense. Possibly he has thought of himself as an immortal, so he has such peculiar ideas. However, all immortals did read! The layman Vimalakirti in Buddhism was merely a layman, why was he respected by many great bodhisattvas such as Manjusri, Samantabhadra and Guanyin? The very reason is that he was a "great gentleman with enormous knowledge". Buddhism pays most attention to wisdom; the knowledge in a secular world does not equate to wisdom, but it is absolutely helpful to the growth of wisdom. Those who advocate that it is not necessary to pursue knowledge is just "anti-intellectualists", and they are as absurd as the "hero who handed in an unanswered paper" in the Cultural Revolution. A man of anti-intellectualism is either foolish or preposterous.

Notes:

1. For such interesting and philosophical remarks of Nan Huaijin, see Liu Yuhong, *The Inside and Outside of the Chan School—A Profile of Mr. Nan Huaijin*（禪門內外——南懷瑾先生側記）, Taipei Lao

Ku Culture Foundation Inc., 1999, 1st edition. Its mainland version is titled *A Profile of Mr. Nan Huaijin*, Beijing Shishi Publishing House, 2001.

2. According to the Consciousness-only Theory (唯識論）, a man has six basic kinds of negative mentalities: greed, anger, ignorance, arrogance, doubt and wrong views, which produce various other afflictions. So these six kinds of mentalities are also called "serious afflictions". Arrogance is just the fourth of these "serious afflictions". This kind of afflictions can be sub-divided into seven types, so it is very complicated. For details, see the author's work *Selection of Buddhist Doctrines* (佛學別裁）, Chapter Three titled "One Hundred Dharma", Section Two.

3. As for the details about "five precepts", see the author's *"Fundamentals of Precept Studies"* (戒律學原理）, p. 258 and infra, Taiwan Lao Ku Culture Foundation Inc., 1999, 1st edition; and the *Buddhist Precepts Studies* (佛教戒律學）, p. 194 and infra, Beijing Religious Culture Publishing House, 2003, 3rd print run.

4. Early modern philosophers in the West recognized Confucius, Sakyamuni, Jesus and Socrates as the four initiators of human cultures, so these four people are called "paradigmatic individuals". See Jaspers K. (1883-1969), *"The Great Philosophers"*, translated by Lai Xianbang, Taipei Jiuda Cultural Company, 1992, 3rd edition.

5. According to official information provided by the CPC, Li Hongzhi has only a junior middle school diploma. See the *Disclose and Criticize the Cult of "Falun Dafa"* (揭批法輪功邪說）, p. 63, Xinhua Publishing House, 1st edition in July 1999.

6. See the *Falun Fofa—Essentials for Further Advances* (Vol. Two), p. 31.

Foolish Mirages

As it is mentioned above, Li Hongzhi likes to be the teacher of others but knows nothing about modesty, and even knows nothing about politeness. That is still trivial in comparison. What is really a serious problem is that he likes to teach others but knows nothing about how to be a teacher. The concrete signs are as the following: 1. His defiant attitude towards the teachers who taught him; and 2. His overbearing and arbitrary attitude towards his "disciples".

He Himself Fabricates Myths

Li Hongzhi admits that he has been instructed by several masters, too, but he created an uncanny myth as such:

"Actually, the things that my several masters taught me in this life are what I deliberately gave them several incarnations ago; when it happened to be the occasion, I arranged them to pass on these things to me in turn, hence enlightened the whole of my dharma." ①

It is really surprising that those several masters who taught Li Hongzhi had been assigned several lives ago by Li Hongzhi to teach him something in this life in turn! In this way, the true master is still Li Hongzhi himself anyhow, and those who play the role of masters to Li Hongzhi in this life are merely Li's tools! Both past and present, at home and abroad, is there any other myth as ridiculous as such on earth?

All religious scriptures inevitably record some myths. For examples, in the *Old Testament* of the *Bible*, there is the tale of Adam and Eve, and in the *New Testament* there are such miracles as Jesus cured lepers; Taoism has the *Stories about Immortals*, and more remarkably, Buddhism has such sutras as the *Jataka Sutra*, which relate many stories of the Buddha in his previous lives. But no matter what religion it is, all such myths were written by others (mostly by disciples of later generations), absolutely not by the protagonists in the myths. Both in the past and at present, at home and abroad, Li Hongzhi is really the only one of his kind who establishes myths and impersonates the protagonist himself.

The Chinese Culture Respects Teachers and Values the Tao

The Chinese nation has been attaching much importance to "what makes a teacher" since the very remotest times, and hence formed the 5,000 years culture which is able to prosper so much and last so long. Confucius was respected as the most important saint of the Chinese nation just because he was "a paragon for numerous generations". Why do the Chinese people respect teachers so much? Let's have a look at a remark of Wang Fu （王符85?-163?), a man of the Han Dynasty (漢朝):

> *"What the Heaven and the Earth value are the greatly virtuous men; what the greatly virtuous men respect are virtue and righteousness; what the virtue and righteousness consummate is intelligence, and what the intelligence pursues is knowledge. Even a greatly virtuous man is not born learned, and even the most intellectual is not born able. So the ancient literature says, 'Emperor Yellow learned from Fengyou, Zhuanxu learned from Laopeng, Emperor Ku learned from Rong, Yao learned from Wucheng, Shun learned from Jihou, Yu learned from Heishi, Tang learned from Yiyin, both King Wen and King Wu learned from Jiang Shang, Duke of Zhou learned from*

*Shuji, and Confucius learned from Laodan.' If these words are authentic, it is clear that a man cannot do without a teacher. Those eleven people were all greatly virtuous, but they still needed to learn despite their high intelligence and great virtue, what would happen to an ordinary man if he does not?" (On Potential Men*潛夫論*)*②

Li Hongzhi, however, surprisingly professes that the teachers who taught him were all that he had arranged in his previous lives; such remarks are the ultimate disesteem to teachers, and also indicate that he has no idea of "respecting teachers and valuing the Tao"; what he respects is only himself, and what he values is only his nonsense.

Certainly, Li Hongzhi would not accept the above refutation and analysis, for he is accustomed to arguing that the so-called "respecting teachers and valuing the Tao" are merely "the idea in a mediocre people's society", how can they be used to criticize his "cosmic law"? The question is, however, Li's various kinds of nonsense are all talked in this "society" to the "mediocre people", they certainly have to receive the test of related regulations of the mediocre people's society. If Li Hongzhi were really a man of ability, who is able to know and assign the matters of previous lives, he should have performed some miracles just as Jesus did; only in this way will the human society not suspect that he is merely a boastful cheater. If he cannot demonstrate his great ability to "arrange his several previous lives" by performing miracles, then all his arguments in the human society would be invalid, and no one of sanity would believe him.

Ignorant of the Way of a Teacher

Li Hongzhi does not know how to respect a teacher, nor does he know how to be a teacher. Then, how to be a teacher? Just as a chapter titled the Exhortation to Study in the *Writings of Xunzi* (荀子) says, "*Qing* (青a kind of blue pigment) is made of *lan* (藍 another kind of blue pigment), but is bluer than *lan*; ice comes out of water, but is colder than water." Any teachers who are really good wish their students to be marvelous, for only when a disciple surpasses his teacher can the teacher be glorified and human culture thus progress. Or otherwise, if students of generations are limited within a confine and are not allowed to get out of the circle one single step, the academic cause would certainly decline generation by generation, and the culture would naturally degenerate. Of course, such a situation is impossible, for man has both his initiative and creativity; if there were a master as such, he must be a fool who does not deserve the title of teacher. But now, here is an idiot like this, and he is Li Hongzhi, the master of "Falun Gong".

Li Hongzhi always stresses that he is the only "master", and prescribes that what he says are "scriptures", that any of his "disciples" shall not change one single word of them, and that the later generations of disciples can only exactly follow them too. This is an extremely arbitrary mentality, and more of an idiotic anti-evolution mentality which is seldom seen in the world.

An Extremely Arbitrary Mentality

As for this issue, Li has repeatedly warned and threatened his "disciples" in his several "Dafa" works; that indicates he is serious about this matter. Let's quote some passages from his original texts:

"My disciples, do remember that all the scriptures about Falun Dafa are the Fa (dharma) that I lecture on, and are what I myself revised and collated, no one shall make excerpts or collate materials in writing from my dharma-preaching records any more. It would be disordering the dharma no matter what excuses it is on, including the so-called collation of the difference between lectures and writings.

*Every step that I Li Hongzhi takes will be an unchangeable pattern prescribed for the spread of Dafa, such great Fa is not a vogue that ends soon, so there cannot be any mistakes at any time. Similarly, the disciples of Dafa are responsible to take the turn to protect Dafa, because it belongs to all the living beings in the universe, including you."*③

"You must understand that the cultivation pattern that I leave with you is unchangeable, you shall not do what I do not, you shall not use what I do not, and you shall talk in the way I talk in the practice. Take care! To change Fofa without noticing it is to destroy it the same way." ④

"I hope all disciples destroy immediately on site the things they privately spread rather than I publicly issued...as well as all the speech drafts, audio records and video records that they privately collated, these things shall not be kept on any excuse. What is to protect Dafa? This is just the thorough protection of Dafa, a standard to test whether the disciples can do as I tell them and whether they are really my disciples! I tell you once again, everyone, Sakyamuni's Dharma had just been destroyed in this way, and that is lesson from the history. From now on, nobody shall make audio or video records of any words talked by any heads of Dafa organizations or any disciples in any places, let alone collating them in writing or spreading them to read and watch." ⑤

"The disciples of Dafa do remember that it will be the disorder of Fa no matter who divide Dafa into different sects in any place at any time on any excuse. What I have not taught you, you can never do; the mentality of brag mixed with that of pleasure may most easily fall into victims of the mentality of devils. Whatever you come to know about Dafa are merely a bit of the principles of the endless Fa at a certain level, be sure not to thus define the Fa, not even a part or a single sentence of it. If you preach publicly, you will commit sins once the words leave your lips. Such sins will be as heavy as mountains or the sky sometimes, how could you cultivate yourself anymore? Those who juggle Dafa and invent another set of teachings will commit enormous sins; they will suffer from endless agony when their life is eroded little by little in the course of remedy of their sins." ⑥

"My disciples! It has been the utmost mercy to human beings that I have reiterated Dafa to the people. This is an unprecedented event for millions of millions of years! Some people, however, still do not treasure it, some people even attempt to revise the Fa or actions and turn them into the possession of their own, of their nations, or of their countries. Just think about it! Any slight revision has committed deadly sins. Be sure not to have any evil impulse for any entice from the mediocre people's society! It is too dangerous!...Some learners suddenly died recent years, I wonder if you know that some of them died just because they had done so." ⑦

The above quotations from Li Hongzhi's texts can be summarized as the following four points:

1. He professes that his own writings are "scriptures", that the "Dafa" that he preaches is just in these scriptures, and that nobody except him shall change one single word. More than that, even to "excerpt" and "collate materials in writing" is not allowed, either. All such actions are the "disordering of the Fa" and should be severely forbidden. —This is an extremely arbitrary mentality.

2. The "Dafa" and its "pattern of practice" in his terms are not allowed to be changed by anyone at present, nor in the future even thousands of generations later.—This is an absurd mirage.

3. The "disciples" at present and in the future must exactly follow what Li Hongzhi has prescribed to practice. No "definition" or explanation is allowed in the future.—This is a stupid idea against evolution and civilization.

4. If "disciples" do not abide by the above-mentioned prescription, they will commit "heavy sins" and risk "extreme dangers". Some people just "suddenly died" recent years that way.—This is a serious threat and hint of violence.

The Cause of Extinguishment of Buddhism in India

In order to rationalize his absurd ideas, Li Hongzhi has also distorted a piece of history of Buddhism as follows:

"Some Buddhist monastics explained Sakyamuni's doctrines this way and that, and some others preached their own thoughts rather than Sakyamuni's, professing that they were Sakyamuni's teachings. That made Fofa distorted beyond recognition, which was not the doctrines that Sakyamuni had preached at all; at the end, the Fofa in Buddhism thus vanished in India. This is important lesson of history; hence there was no Buddhism in India instead later on. Buddhism had experienced several reforms before it disappeared; finally it combined something of Brahmanism, forming a kind of religion prevalent in today's India, which is called Hinduism. It does not worship the Buddha anymore; instead, it worships something else; nor does it believe in Sakyamuni anymore. That is what the case is." ⑧

Buddhism did not vanish as Li Hongzhi explains; instead, it is a result of such political cause as the Turkic and Persian Islam forces' invasion into India. So, what Li says above is not the fact at all.

Actually, Buddhism split into sects step by step after the passing of Sakyamuni, and there was mainly the opposition between two major sects (Sthaviravada [Teaching of the Elders] and Mahasaghikah [Great Sangha]). Later on, these two major sects continued to split; by one hundred years after the Buddha's nirvana, there had been as many as 20 sects. This piece of history is called "the sectarian period of Buddhism". This period lasted about 300 years; at its end, i.e., around the four hundredth year after the Buddha's passing, Mahayana Buddhism sprang up. This Mahayana Buddhism lasted four hundred years, too, and this period is called "the period of Mahayana Buddhism". By the 8th century, Esoteric Buddhism became the major sect of Buddhism in India, and thus began the "Age of Esoteric Buddhism". This period also lasted four hundred years.

The Buddhism in India lingered on in a steadily worsening condition until A. D. 1202 when Islam forces from the west swept North India. The next year, the Vikramasila Monastery, the center of Esoteric Buddhism, was burnt down by Muslims, and the Buddhist monastics over there fled away. This event marked the formal end of Buddhism in India after it lasted 1,600 years.⑨

What should be kept in mind is that the split of Buddhism into many sects after the nirvana of the Buddha was a necessary result of the development of man's spiritual civilization, and such split did no harm to the development of Buddhism afterwards, instead, it enriched the content of Buddhism; it was absolutely not that such split caused the destruction of Buddhism as Li Hongzhi has asserted. It is really puerile that Li attempts to rationalize his absurd mentality by faking the history of Buddhism.

The Rule of Cultural Development

Any great thought or culture must experience the supplementation and development by talents of later generations before they become great. This is the law of development of civilizations of man. The Buddhism after the Buddha's nirvana had been enriched and developed by numerous virtuous Buddhists before it turned out to be a world religion. Laotze's doctrines developed into brilliant Taoist culture thanks to the explanations by Zhuangzi（莊子）, the Taoists, alchemists and sorcerers of the Qin (221—206 B.C.) and Han (202 B.C.—220 A.D.) dynasties, and the masters of the Metaphysics of the Wei (220—266 A.D.) and Jin (266—420 A.D.) dynasties. And Confucius, who has been viewed as the most typical Confucian thinker, is a more conspicuous example of this kind: He depends upon the common efforts of later generations to become the kernel spirit of the Chinese culture, including Zengzi(曾子), Zisi(子思), Mencius, Xunzi(荀子) and even the great thinkers of the School of Principles(理学) of the Song (960--1276) and Ming (1368--1644) dynasties such as the Cheng Brothers(二程夫子), Zhu Xi(朱熹), Lu Jiuyuan(陸九渊), Wang Yangming(王陽明) and so forth. Furthermore, Jesus Christ, who established a religion in the name of God, could hardly have become a god of "trinity" without the hermeneutic and extol by Paul and other disciples as well as followers of later generations such as St. Augustine (354-430) and Thomas Aguina (1225-1274).

Therefore, any attempt to keep one's things (body, power, wealth, writings and so on) unchanged forever is an opposition against the law of development of civilizations of human beings, an opposition to the principle of "non-eternalness" in Buddhism, and it is an extremely selfish and foolish mirage. Qin Shi Huang (秦始皇259 B. C.—210 B.C.) impractically attempted to preserve his power for endless generations, but it perished as soon as by the second generation. He turned out to be a butt of political jokes for later generations. Now, Li Hongzhi is ranting on about guaranteeing his "Dafa" "not to go slightly astray even up to ten thousand generations later". It is a kind of religious ineptitude. What result will it lead to? It has been obvious already without divination.

Notes:

1. *Essentials for Further Advances*, pp. 61-62.
2. Quoted from the *Imperial Readings of the Taiping Era*（太平御覽）, Vol. 404, p. 8
3. *Essentials for Further Advances*, pp. 63-64.
4. Ibid, p. 106.
5. Ibid, p. 109.
6. Ibid, p. 117.
7. Ibid, p. 97.
8. *Zhuan Falun*, p. 109.
9. For details of the ruin of Buddhism in India, see Yu Lingbo（于淩波）, the *Concise Outline of Buddhism*（簡明佛學概論）, Chapter 2, The Grand East Book Co., Ltd., Taipei, 1999; the author's *Selection of Buddhist Doctrines*, Chapter 8.

Who Is Plagiarizing
"Dharma" (Doctrines)?

Li Hongzhi wrote an essay titled "Dafa Can Never Be Plagiarized", which sternly forbids his "disciples" to make any revision on his "Dafa":

> *"My disciples! It has been the utmost mercy to human beings that I have reiterated Dafa to the people. This is an unprecedented event for millions of millions of years! Some people, however, still do not treasure it, some people even attempt to revise the Fa (dharma or doctrines) or actions and turn them into the possession of their own...This is the cosmic law, the very foundation of Fofa! ...Any slight revision means deadly sins already. Be sure not to have any evil impulse for any entice from the mediocre people's society! It is too dangerous!...Some learners suddenly died recent years, I wonder if you know that some of them died just because they had done so."*①

Li's "disciples" would be plagiarizing the "Fa (doctrines)" if they dare to change a bit of his words, and the cost would be their death! Such a threat is rather frightening! Another essay titled "Awakening" contains words with similar meanings, and its tone is more arrogant:

*"Disciples, do keep in your mind that all the scriptures about Falun Dafa are the doctrines that I speak out, are revised and collated by myself, no one shall excerpt or collate any materials in writing from the audio records of my lectures on such doctrines; no matter on what excuse it is, it is the distortion of the Fa."*②

In Li Hongzhi's other writings there are still many passages like the above quoted two, here the author does not take trouble to quote more. These two passages are laughable enough to any people of insights. Is it not a typical means to "cover oneself by shouting with the crowd"?! The so-called all "scriptures" in Li's term are mostly terms and theories plagiarized from Buddhism, and the rest are plagiarized from Taoism. He mixes these glossaries with scientific terms (such as the universe, the Galaxy, particles, quarks and so on) frequently seen in newspapers and journals, stretching their meanings to make his nonsense. He himself is a real plagiarist and destroyer of doctrines, but now he threatens others in a harsh tone and with a severe expression not to plagiarize or distort the Fa. Is it not extremely ridiculous?

What Is Fofa?

Is the "Fofa" (Buddhist Dharma or Buddhist doctrines) in Li Hongzhi's term really Fofa on earth? In order to answer this question, let's make it clear what Fofa (佛法) is.

The Buddhist term "dharma" has complicated meanings,③ hence the term "Fofa" can be explained in many ways. But its basic meaning, that is, the comprehension of common people in their common sense is evident: the so-called "Fofa" is just the doctrines or truths in Buddhism, or to say, it is the truths that the Buddha (Sakyamuni or Tathagata [如來the Thus-Come]) had taught.

Then, what are the "doctrines of Buddhism"?

All Buddhist doctrines are represented through the Tripitaka. Each part of the extant Tripitaka consists of more than ten thousand volumes, which is really a huge number; so it is both impossible and unnecessary to talk about the doctrines of Buddhism in details right here. But Buddhism has "*san fa yin*"(三法印) (literally three seals of the dharma or three marks of the law), which are three basic criteria to distinguish Buddhism from other schools of thoughts, and they are what readers have to be familiar with.

Three Seals of the Dharma

The so-called "seals of the dharma" means the verification of Buddhist doctrines. The ancient Chinese people were accustomed to impressing seals on things that have been verified for evidence. So, the "three seals of the dharma" are just three principles or criteria to distinguish "the correct" from "the incorrect" within Buddhism.

1. All Things Are Impermanent: All conditioned things are brought into being by "causes or causation". They cannot exist forever after they come into being; instead, they have to go through the course of "arising" (生), "abiding" (住), "changing" (異) and "extinction" (滅) (also known as formation, existence, destruction and void).

2. All Things Lack Inherent Existence (Non-self): All things, no matter whether they are material or spiritual, are in lack of "self" (the essence of itself). In other words, all things are formed with various causes, and there is not such a thing as a thing-in-itself. This nature is known as "emptiness".

3. Nirvana Is Perfect Quintessence: Mediocre people misunderstand the "impermanence" of things as "permanence", and mistake the "non-self" as the availability of "self"; the clinging to such ideas of "permanence" and "self" causes endless affliction. Through correct cognition and practices, such mistaken pertinacity can be eradicated, and a tranquil realm would thus emerge, which is just the realm of "nirvana", and is characterized with permanence, pleasure, selfhood and purity. A person in this stage would attain the achievements of saints (arhat, bodhisattvas and Buddhas) step by step.

Li Hongzhi Does Not Know the True Meaning of "Emptiness"

With an overall exhaustion of Li Hongzhi's "Fofa", one can say that it has nothing in compliance with the criterion of "three seals of the dharma". For example, his comprehension of "emptiness" is surprisingly as follows:

> *"The Thus-Come said that kong (emptiness, or sunya in Sanskrit) is actually that there are totally not the thoughts of ordinary people, and wulou (uncontaminated, literally "no-outflow", or anasrava in Sanskrit) is the truth of emptiness. The universe is actually a space where materials exist, form and belong to, how can it be empty?"*④

The concept *"kong"* (空emptiness) is the most fundamental one in Buddhism. In Buddhism, the so-called "emptiness" does not mean that nothing exists (nothingness); instead, it means that all existences depend upon causes, and there is no "self" or "self-nature" as a thing-in-itself. For example, when we say that "this car is empty", we do not mean that this car does not exist; instead, what we mean is that this car is not a thing-in-itself. Why do we say so? Because this car is a result of piles of parts and other factors such as workers' job and factories. We call it a "car", but it is that there is really a "car as a thing-in-itself" existing there. Once these parts (carriage, wheels and so forth) are taken apart, the car itself will not exist anymore. For another example, Li Hongzhi as a "person" does not exist because of the existence of *"yuan shen"* (元神original spirit) or *"fu yuan shen"* (副元神secondary original spirit) as he has blathered; instead, it is a mere combination of his mind and body (sensation [Vedana], perception [Samjna], mental formations [Samskara] and consciousness [Vijnana]), which are called "five clusters" (五蘊skandhas in Sanskrit) in Buddhism. It is Li's most serious "obduracy" to mistake that he has a "self" as the thing-in-itself (original spirit or soul), and imagine for himself that there would be a "self alone" a hundred years later. Such "obduracy" is the source of all afflictions, which is just what Buddhism intends to eliminate. It proves that Li knows nothing about the most important and the most basic doctrine of Buddhism, and that his obduracy is much more serious than common people.

Moreover, *"wulou"*（無漏） and *"kong"* （空）are two completely different concepts in Buddhism. *"Lou"*（漏） is the translation of a Sanskrit word "asrava" into Chinese, which alludes to "contamination" or "affliction", while *"kong"* suggests that all existences depend upon causes and have no selves; these two concepts are related indeed (It is possible to eliminate afflictions only after the doctrine of emptiness is understood), but it is not that "one is the truth of the other". Evidently Li does not know much about Buddhism. He often alleges that "The universe is actually a space where materials exist, develop and belong to, how can it be empty". This indicates that he does know the meaning of *"kong"* at all, that is why he gives such remarks opposite to Fofa (Buddhist doctrines).

In a word, such idea of *"kong"* is the true meaning of the 1st and 2nd points of the above-mentioned "three seals of the dharma", and also the highest and the most fundamental doctrine of Fofa. That is why Buddhism is also called *"kongmen"* （空門） in Chinese language. Not understanding such meaning of "emptiness", one cannot be viewed as has truly understood Fofa. If misunderstanding and even distorting the meaning of *"kong"*, one would be completely a Papiyan⑤ who is against Buddhism although he still professes to hold the banner of "Fofa".

The Secret of Deception and Hypocrisy

As above-quoted Li's remarks show, he obviously does not know the meaning of *"kong"*, and that is why he takes the word literally and talks nonsense. Worse than that, he thinks his "Dafa" is even superior to Buddhism and Taoism:

"What Buddhism expounds is merely the weakest and the smallest part of Fofa: All Living Beings! Don't estimate the Dafa of Truthfulness, Compassion, and Forbearance with the standpoint of Buddhism, for the former is beyond any estimate...When Taoists mention Taiji, they likewise merely cognize the universe at a lower level...The Thus-Come's words are the representation of Buddhahood, so they can be viewed as the embodiment of Fa, too, but it is not the substantial Fa

*of the universe...Falun Dafa is the first to reveal the qualities (Fofa) of the universe to human beings since the very remotest times, it is as if it has left a set of stairs leading to the Heaven. So, how can you judge the cosmic law with things in the obsolete Buddhism?"*⑥

This passage can be paraphrased as such: The doctrines that the Buddha taught can only be viewed as "the representation of Fa" (a thing-in-itself can have various representations, so a representation is not so important), and is not the highest and essential Fa of the universe yet; only Falun Gong is the "cosmic law", i.e., the highest Dafa surpassing Fofa. How arrogant and how ignorant these remarks are! It would be the breach deserving Parajika if in the circle of Buddhists.⑦

Again, Li says,

*"The Fa (doctrines) in the Buddhism cannot be equated with the whole Fofa, for it is a very small part of Fofa...For the practices of Truthfulness, Compassion and Forbearance, Taoism lays an emphasis on Truthfulness...Buddhism lays an emphasis on Compassion. Our Falun Dafa follows the highest standard of the universe—the simultaneous practice of Truthfulness, Compassion and Forbearance, so the Gong (actions) we practice is very great."*⑧

*"The principles that Sakyamuni and Laotze talked in their times are all those within the scope of our Galaxy. Then, what does our Falun Dafa practice? We are practicing in the light of the principle of evolution of the universe, we are taking the highest qualities of the universe—Truthfulness, Compassion and Forbearance as a standard to direct our practices. Now that we are practicing such a great thing, it equates to that we are practicing the universe."*⑨

These two passages clearly indicate that although Li Hongzhi keeps talking "the Buddha" and "the Tao", he thinks that he is more transcendent and more consummate than Laotze in China and the Buddha in India, so the so-called "Fofa" and the "practice of the Tao" in his terms are not the doctrines of traditional Buddhism or Taoism at all.

Obviously, it is a mixture of arrogance, deception and hypocrisy. Li plagiarizes a lot of Buddhist and Taoist terms on the one hand, and professes that his Falun Gong is different from Buddhism and Taoism (more transcendent and greater than the latter two) on the other hand. So, it is no wonder many people can hardly see through the secret of Falun Gong.

Notes:
1. *Essentials for Further Advances*, p. 97.
2. Ibid, p. 61.
3. The Chinese character "*fa*" (法) is a translation of Sanskrit word "Dharma", and has a large scope of meanings. It can refer to the existence of all things (in the sense of ontology), the nature, qualities, attributes or other aspects of things (in the sense of epistemology), or rules, laws, virtue and characters (in the sense of criteria). And also, it can refer to the objects and predications in the structure of a sentence (in the sense of Buddhist logic). As for this question, see Wu Rujun, the *Buddhist Thoughts Dictionary* (吳汝鈞: 佛教思想大辭典), the entry of "fa". Taiwan Commercial Press, 1994.
4. *Essentials for Further Advances*, p. 17.
5. Papiyan (波旬), a devil in Buddhist sutras, who intently ruins Fofa.
6. *Essentials for Further Advances*, p. 19.
7. "Parajika" (波羅夷) is the most severe punishment in Buddhism, which means to expel a Buddhist out of Sangha. In the light of related provisions in Buddhism, those who commit the four heavy

sins of improper sex, killing, steal and groundless remarks will receive "Parajika" as a punishment, that is, to be expelled out of Sangha and never to be admitted as a Buddhist anymore. In particular, the fourth kind of crime "groundless remarks" refers to severe deception related the degree of cultivation, such as to "profess to have attained some achievements while actually having not", or to "cheat others by professing to have supernatural abilities while actually having no such abilities." For this question, see the author's *Fundamentals of Precept Studies* (each section in Chapter 8), Taipei Lao Ku Culture Foundation Inc., 2001, 2nd edition; the author's *Buddhist Precepts Studies*, Beijing Religious Culture Publishing House, 2002, 3rd print run.
8. *Zhuan Falun*, p. 18.
9. Ibid, p. 45.

A Cock-and-Bull Story about "Falun"

So to speak, the term "Falun" is the kernel concept in Li Hongzhi's "Dafa", and his "Falun Gong" thus got its name, too. This term, however, was not invented by Li Hongzhi himself; actually, Li plagiarizes it from Taoism and uses it to allude to Buddhism.

Originally, "*falun*" was a term in Buddhism; later on, Taoism borrowed it to refer to a kind of practice method. Let's make clear its meaning from the point of Buddhist doctrines at first, and then have a look at its usage in Taoism, and at last refute and analyze Li Hongzhi's fantastic story.

The Original Meaning of Falun

Sakyamuni got enlightened six years after he left home. Afterwards, he preached for more than 40 years, which has been called "*zhuan fa lun*"(轉法輪). Here, the word "*zhuan*" means to "turn like a wheel", "*fa*" refers to the Buddha's instruction (mainly the truth of suffering [dukkha], the truth of the arising of suffering [samudaya], the truth of the cessation of suffering [nirodha], and the truth of the path to the cessation of suffering [marga]), which are called "Four Noble Truths" (四聖諦), and "*lun*" is just a "wheel", and also a simile to allude to "Cakravarti-raja".

Actually, there went tales about "Cakravarti-raja" in ancient India, just like the "sacred kings" (聖王) in the ancient China, who were the symbol of ideal politics. Such great monarchs lived in this world to perform benevolent politics, just as a turning wheel could carry a cart to a far distance, and the multitude thus benefited from their virtue and lived a happy life. The true dharma spread by Sakyamuni was not a political "wheel", but it was more helpful to the living beings, that is, it was a "wheel" to teach people how to eliminate endless afflictions, therefore it was called "*falun*". "Falun" is also known as "*fanlun*" (梵輪magnificent wheel), it often employs the mark "卍" to express the meaning of "ceaseless turning of wheels".

The above-mentioned can be found in the *Mahaprajnaparamita Sastra* (大智度論), Vol. 8, which says,

> "*The Buddha turns a Falun. Some people call it Falun, and some others call it Fanlun.*"
> "*The Buddha turns the Falun, just as a Cakravarti-raja turns a treasure wheel…The Buddha rules all gods and human beings in all worlds with his Falun.*"

Overall, the "Falun" in Buddhism refers to Sakyamuni's instructions, and it is only a figurative term. It was not Sakyamuni who employed this figurative term; rather, it was a term that followers of later generations used to show their esteems to him.

The "Autorotation Practice of Falun" in Taoism

The "Autorotation Practice of Falun" is recorded in the second section of the Volume Heng in *A Genuine Taoist Guide to Cultivation of Nature and Life*, a classic of Taoism.① It largely says as follows: A practitioner should set the conception of a "benevolent mind" on the very center of his body (below the heart and above the navel), which is called "*li ji*" (立極to establish a pole). Then, the practitioner has something imagined turning circle around this pole clockwise, one after another from the interior to the exterior, and from small to large, meanwhile reiterates in silence the 12 Chinese characters "*bai hu yin yu dong fang, qing long qian yu xi wei*" (白虎隐於東方, 青龍潛於西位a white tiger is hidden in the east, and a green dragon is hidden in the west). That something turns one circle when the practitioner recites these 12 characters once, and stops after he turns 36 circles. Immediately after that, he turns in reversed direction (anti-clockwise), from the exterior to the interior, and from large to small. Likewise, each circle is accompanied with a recitation of these 12 words, and the total number of circles should be 36, too. One round of reciprocation as such is called "*yi zhoutian*" (一周天). Turning on intently this way for long, the *falun* in the practitioner's body will turn ceaselessly without being noticed. It is said that such pattern of practice can effect miracles both to mind and body, and there is a poem saying "*The Way of longevity is obtained while in leisure, and the falun is turned on in silence day and night*" (安閑自得長生道, 晝夜無聲轉法輪), which can be taken as evidence.

A Groundless Story

Obviously, Li Hongzhi has plagiarized the practice method of Taoism and the terms of Buddhism, unrestrainedly professing his "Falun Gong" to be "Fofa". In practical exercises, his "Falun Fofa" does not take any trouble as Taoism does to recite a pithy formula; instead, it takes a bit of Christianity pattern—In Christianity, a prayer must be added with an expression "in Jesus' name" at the end, only in this way the prayer can take effects! In Falun Gong, however, what you need to rely on is "Master Li".

How to rely on him, then? According to Li Hongzhi, so long as you listen to his lectures, or watch his video tapes, or even merely read his books, his "reality-bodies" would have embedded a "*falun*" in your *dantian* (丹田 a place in the lower abdomen). This *falun* is really wonderful: When you practice, you are "exercising *falun*" indeed; but when you do not practice, that *falun* will be automatically "practicing you", this is called "a man practices Fa, and the Fa exercises the man in return." This "*falun*" will rotate in your *dantian* forever; it absorbs the energy of the universe while it turns clockwise, and it discharges the waste in your body and gives off energy when it rotates anti-clockwise. When it gives off energy, it will benefit the people around you.

Li Hongzhi repeatedly stresses that practitioners can never be between two stools, and that so long as you intently practice the

"Falun Dafa", your "*gong*" (the power gained through the practice of "Falun Gong") will increase day after day. If you mix "Falun Dafa" with things from Buddhism or Taoism the other way round, your "*falun*" will be deformed, and cannot be cultivated anymore.

So long as you practice the five sets of actions in the light of Li Hongzhi's "Dafa", you will attain "true achievements" (正果) by certain moments (an earlier or later moment depends upon the particular conditions of practitioners), and you will foster a "*falun*" of your own. But no matter how hard you try, you can never reach such a transcendent degree as "Master Li" has done, because he has numberless "reality-bodies", and each "reality-body" of his is an independent body, and is able to exercise supernatural force all over the universe. Now that you are an ordinary man, it has been very marvelous already if you can attain a bit supernatural ability through cultivation, so be sure not to impractically expect to reach the level of the "Master".

That is largely the content of the "cock and bull story about Falun".

Now, let's quote some original text of Li Hongzhi's lectures, so that readers appreciate them.

> *"This set of our practice methods is to foster a falun in the lower abdomen, and I myself embed them for trainees at each training class. When I lecture on Falun Dafa, we embed falun for each of you in succession, some people can feel it, and some others cannot, this is because people's physical conditions differ. We cultivate falun instead of dan (丹 pills of immortality in Taoism); falun is a miniature of the universe, and has all the functions of the universe—it is able to operate and rotate by itself. It rotates in the lower abdomen forever; once it is embedded in your lower abdomen, it will not stop anymore--It will turn on forever... because it turns ceaselessly, constantly absorbing energy from the universe and evolving energy. When you are on duty, it is cultivating you. It is not limited to falun, of course; we embed many other functions and mechanisms in your bodies, which all automatically operate and evolve together with falun. So, this*

Gong totally automatically evolves practitioners. In this way, it forms a situation in which "the Gong exercises a practitioner", or "the Fa exercises a practitioner". When you do not exercise, the Gong exercises you; when you practice the Gong, it exercises you, too. No matter if you are eating, sleeping or on duty, you are always in the evolution of the Gong. What do you practice the Gong for? You practice the Gong in order to hold the falun, and hold all the functions and qi that I embedded in you."②

The above passage is addressed to those who participated in "Education Classes" (the occasion on which Li Hongzhi himself gives lectures). Then, what about the others who do not attend such classes? Are they able to obtain "*falun*"? Li alleges as follows,

"I've explained this question for many times. To read books has the same effect; so long as you really exercise in the light of Dafa, there would be no problem even if you live in the remotest place alone. Our books contain my reality-bodies; from the point of view at a lower level, each word is in the size of falun, it knows everything in your mind. It is the same; you can attain it so long as you really can practice it. You can practice it by reading books, or go to exercise sites to practice together with veteran practitioners. You can obtain it so long as you really cultivate yourself."③

So long as you exercise in the light of what Li Hongzhi has taught you, you will own a "*falun*" at the end, but you can never expect to have one as large as that of Li Hongzhi. So, he says again,

"After our trainees obtain true achievements in the future, they can develop their own falun, but each of you can develop only one falun. You can have only one falun even if you have reached a very high level, and that falun is your own representation; it will substitute for the falun that I gave in the lower abdomen, and that is your true fruit. But falun is also the representation of Fa, and it can split; when you exercise supernatural force, it

can split. You can give off some falun, but you cannot give off so many independent entities as I have cultivated today...It is impossible for you to develop such huge things as I have done in the course of practice, absolutely impossible."④

As the above quotations show, Li Hongzhi's theory about "*falun*" is not only a cock-and-bull story, but also it is really promoting a kind of superstition. This kind of superstition is very special; it is not a common kind of superstition which promotes the idea of ghosts or gods; rather, it wants Falun Gong disciples to have superstitions about Li Hongzhi himself.

The Meaning of Mixin (Superstition)

When we talk "*mixin*" (迷信superstition), we should make clear the meaning of the word "*mixin*" (superstition) by the way. Li Hongzhi is very sensitive to the term "superstition" probably because there have been a lot of remarks criticizing "Falun Gong" to be superstitious, and he has specially published two essays respectively titled "What Is Superstition" and "Another Discussion on Superstition",⑤ intending to contradict people's criticism.

Surprisingly, Li alleges that literally *mixin* (superstition) has nothing wrong because *"what the word 'mixin' (superstition) is not a bad thing, for military men will have no battle effectiveness if they are not superstitious about disciplines, students cannot acquire knowledge if they are not superstitious about schools or teachers, children cannot be fostered if they are not superstitious about their parents...".* That evidently shows Li completely does not understand the word "*mixin*" (superstition), and he is just talking nonsense by taking the word literally. How can military men's abidance by disciplines, students' respect to teachers and children's obedience to their parents be viewed as any "superstition"? Possibly Li Hongzhi is the only one in the world who dares to talk such nonsense!

Consulting any Chinese dictionaries, one can find the Chinese character "*mi*" in the expression "*mixin*" means "confusion", which is opposite to "reason". So, the word "*mixin*" (superstition) absolutely does not mean "absolute trust or belief", rather, it is the opposition to "proper conviction", and is absolutely a derogatory term. Li Hongzhi even employs sophism for such a simple word, so we can imagine how low his level is. He professes that it is not superstition, but whoever can believe him?

Li Hongzhi Apotheosizes Himself

At last, there is another extremely severe question that should be put up. Li alleges that other people cannot reach his realm no matter how they practice; this is a bad "anti-humanism" thought, and is completely opposite to the ethos of Chinese culture.

The Confucianism in China elevated "benevolence" （仁） to the highest level, viewing it as the way of the Heaven, and its ideal representatives were Yao （堯） and Shun （舜）, but anyone could become Yao and Shun so long as he gave a full play to his "conscience" （良知）. This is the kernel thought of Confucianism. So it is with Buddhism. In Buddhism, "Buddhahood" is at the highest level, but everyone has the "nature of Buddhahood", and everyone can become a Buddha so long as he makes arduous efforts to practice and completely shake off "ignorance" （無明）. Taoist thoughts are complicated in comparison, but Taoism as a whole also thinks that everyone can reach the realm of reality and immortality so long as he practices, so it is similar with Confucianism and Buddhism. Only the Christianity from the West is different. In Christianity, God is just "truth, path and life", and represents the absolute and final truth in the universe. A human being cannot reach the realm of God through practice, the only way to be saved is to believe in Jesus, and only in this way can a person's soul go to the Heaven after his death. Although his soul has gone to the Heaven, still he cannot become a God.⑥

Li Hongzhi imprudently alleges that his "*falun*" cannot be obtained by others through "practice". Let's put aside how absurd his idea of "*falun*" is for the moment, when we have a look at this mentality, we can find that he has viewed himself as God. He professes to be "God", what is it if it is not superstition? As the history of mankind shows, anyone who professes to be "God" or "Truth" is absolutely an arrogant and unscrupulous person no matter in what sphere it is. Such arrogant and unscrupulous people would certainly cause enormous social disasters at the end if they have a considerable amount of blind followers.

Notes:

1. This book was written about in the early Qing Dynasty (清朝1636--1911) by a Taoist. A fashion of syncretism of Confucianism, Buddhism and Taoism prevailed at that time, therefore this book integrated the doctrines of Confucianism and Buddhism into a Taoist classic. Taiwan: Woolin Publishing Company（武陵出版公司）, 2000, 2nd edition, 2nd print run. Evidently, Li's many conceptions come from this book.

2. *Zhuan Falun*, pp. 46-48.

3. *Falun Dafa Interpretation*, p. 19.

4. Ibid, p. 16.

5. These two essays are respectively published in the *Essentials for Further Advances*, p. 42 and the *Essentials for Further Advances* (Vol. Two), p. 11.

6. The differences between Confucianism, Buddhism, Taoism and Christianity are very complicated; those who are interested may see Mou Zongsan(牟宗三), *Fourteen Lectures on the Convergence of Chinese-Western Philosophies*（中西哲學之會通十四講）. Taiwan: Taipei Student Book Co., Ltd., 1996.

What Is "Truthfulness, Compassion and Forbearance"?

Li Hongzhi's disciples always hold a huge banner which says "Truthfulness, Compassion and Forbearance" no matter what public activities they perform. Usually people think these three words the sign of "Falun Gong", or its spiritual criterion, but Li calls them "the highest qualities of the universe". What do these three words mean on earth? Let's see how Li Hongzhi explains them at first:

> *"What is Fofa? It is Truthfulness, Compassion and Forbearance, which are the most fundamental qualities of this universe, the most advanced representation of Fofa; that is the most fundamental Fofa. Fofa has different forms of representations at different levels, and have different guidance roles at different levels; the lower the level is, the more complicated its representation will be. All materials have such qualities as of Truthfulness, Compassion and Forbearance, including the particles in the air, stones, wood, soil, iron, steel and human bodies. The ancient people held that Five Elements constituted all things in the universe, they all have the attributes of Truthfulness, Compassion and Forbearance."*

"At a highest level it can be generalized with three words, which are just Truthfulness, Compassion and Forbearance, and it becomes complicated when it is represented at other levels."

"So it is with this universe of ours, it consists of the Galaxy, other galactic systems, life and water, as well as all other things in this universe, this is the material aspect of existences; but meantime, it has the attributes of Truthfulness, Compassion and Forbearance. All small particles in all material have such attributes, so it is even with extremely small particles."

Overall, the above three passages actually view "Truthfulness, Compassion and Forbearance" as the ultimate principle of the universe; this is Li's worst mistake in using these three words (see detailed refutation and analysis below).

"Such attributes as Truthfulness, Compassion and Forbearance are the criterion to judge the good and the bad in the universe. What is the good and what is the bad? We just make judgment in the light of these attributes...As a human being, he who can be a good person only if he is able to comply with the attributes of Truthfulness, Compassion and Forbearance of the universe, and he who deviates from such attributes is really a bad one."

This is generalizing these three words as the conduct code of human beings. Then, can "Truthfulness, Compassion and Forbearance" become a sufficient standard to judge a good person or a bad one? This is a controversial question.

"Taoism lays its emphasis on truthfulness when it cultivates Truthfulness, Compassion and Forbearance, so Taoists advocate cultivating truthfulness and human nature, telling the truth, doing truthful things, being truthful men, returning to simplicity and truth, and becoming a Zhenren (true man) at the end. It advocates both forbearance and compassion, too, but its emphasis is on truthfulness. Buddhism lays its emphasis

on compassion. Our Falun Dafa, however, simultaneously practices Truthfulness, Compassion and Forbearance, the highest standard of the universe, so the Gong we practice is very great." ①

"What does our Falun Dafa practice? We practice in the light of the principle of evolution of the universe, and we take Truthfulness, Compassion and Forbearance, the highest qualities of the universe to direct our practice." ②

This is denouncing both Buddhism and Taoism as partial practice, alleging that they are not so consummate and brilliant as Li's "Truthfulness, Compassion and Forbearance".

"Compassion is the representation of qualities of the universe at different levels in different spaces, and is also the basic original nature of the greatly enlightened. So, a practitioner must assimilate the cosmic attributes of Truthfulness, Compassion and Forbearance. Enormous celestial bodies are constituted with the cosmic attributes of Truthfulness, Compassion and Forbearance." ③

The passage above sources from an essay which is titled "A Preliminary Discussion on Compassion", but as a matter of fact, the whole essay contains no single word explaining what "compassion" is.

"Forbearance is the pivot to improve mind and nature. The forbearance with outrage, resentment, grievances and tears means the submission of a mediocre person who has obdurate apprehension in his mind, and only the forbearance without any outrage, resentment or grievances is the forbearance of a practitioner." ④

This passage can be considered as has explained the term "forbearance" anyhow. What deserves attention is that it was published on January 21, 1996.

> *"Forbearance does not mean cowardice, let alone the willing submission to any unwanted things…Forbearance is absolutely not unlimited connivance, which would encourage the evil life that has lost the basic humanity and correct thought to wantonly commit evils…Truthfulness, Compassion and Forbearance are the Fa! They are the representation of the cosmic law at different levels, but they are absolutely not any thought of human beings or any criteria of daily life in the opinion of mediocre people. If evils have grown to an incurable extent, then people are allowed to take any measures at different levels to stop and eradicate them…Fa contains the principle of response beyond endurance…Judging from the evil signs at present, they have lost all their humanity and correct thought, so people cannot endure their evil prosecution against the Fa anymore. The eradication of evils is for the sake of true dharma, not for the cultivation of individuals. Usually, there is not such a question as beyond endurance in the practice of individuals."*

This passage sources from an essay published on January 1, 2001. In this essay titled "Beyond Endurance", Li Hongzhi asks his disciples not to tolerate "evils" anymore, which is exactly opposite to his attitude before. This obviously contradicts the passage quoted just now. In order to cover up such contradiction, Li invents the strangest reason: "Truthfulness, Compassion and Forbearance" are absolutely not the "criteria of daily life", instead, they are the "representation of the cosmic law at different levels".

As for Li Hongzhi's remarks quoted above, the author makes comprehensive refutation and analysis as follows:

1. Any sectarian groups must have their own spiritual or moral criteria that they pursue, or otherwise they cannot continue to survive or develop. For example,

Confucianism makes a favorable publicity of "three universal virtues" (三達德 intelligence, benevolence and bravery), "four dimensions" (四維 sense of propriety, sense of righteousness, sense of honor, and sense of shame), "five constant virtues" (五常 benevolence, righteousness, propriety, intelligence, and sincerity), and "eight virtues" (八德 loyalty, filial piety, benevolence, love, sincerity, righteousness, harmony and peacefulness), which are all good items of virtues to maintain the ethical relations of human beings; the prosperity and development of the Chinese nation that have last thousands of years have proved that such items of virtues are necessary and effective. For another example, Buddhism promotes "four immeasurable states of mind" (四無量心 also called "noble Brahma-acts/characteristics", which are love [maitre], compassion [karuna], sympathetic joy [mudita] and impartiality [upeksa]), which are the underlying items of Buddhist virtues.⑤ And also, the spiritual criteria of Christianity are "Faith, Hope and Love", and in the Greek philosophy there had been the highest moral criteria, namely "four cardinal virtues" (prudence, courage, abstinence and justice). There are still many of such examples, which are unnecessary to numerate one by one. If "Truthfulness, Compassion and Forbearance" were merely considered as the spiritual criteria or interior regulations of "Falun Gong" as a sectarian group, it would be very common, and we would not have much to say about them even if they are questionable. But here the question is that Li has alleged these three words as "the highest qualities of the universe"; that hence turns out to be a serious problem.

2. It involves metaphysics and ontology to view those three words as "the highest qualities of the universe". The western philosophy has its source in the ancient Greece.

Tales (624 B.C. or so—545 B.C.), the first philosopher in the ancient Greece, held that water was the highest principle of the universe, and the basic elements constituting all things in the world. Afterwards, there emerged several other philosophers who tried to explain the complicated phenomena of the universe with such simple principles as "water, fire, earth and air". By the time of Plato (427-347 B.C.), he argued that there was a thing-in-itself called "idea" behind all the various phenomena in the universe. According to Plato, what we human beings could perceive were mere phenomena; phenomena varied and changed easily, but ideas were an unchangeable metaphysical structure. In 2,000 years from then on, many western philosophers were trapped in the metaphysics that pursues the "highest qualities of the universe", debating and arguing in succession. This situation did not change until Immanuel Kant (1724—1840), a great German philosopher in the early modern times; people hence did not research that ancient question anymore, instead, they turned towards the fundamental of knowledge of us human beings and the limit and capacity of our "ability to know". As results have proven, those metaphysical ultimate questions about the universe are beyond man's cognitive ability. Now, Li Hongzhi proposes that "Truthfulness, Compassion and Forbearance" are the ultimate principle of the universe, is he trying to imitate the philosophers of the ancient Greece? It seems that he has no such ability. The ancient Greek philosophers reasoned about and demonstrated their opinions no matter what they put forwards; but Li offered no single word of reasoning, simply alleging that "Truthfulness, Compassion and Forbearance are the highest qualities of the universe". Hence, his opinion is not a philosophical view but some superstition or nonsense.

3. Even if "Truthfulness, Compassion and Forbearance" are considered the spiritual or moral norms of Falun Gong, it is still questionable. Why does Li Hongzhi choose these three words? According to himself, Taoism lays an emphasis on the cultivation of "truthfulness", and Buddhism lays an emphasis on that of "compassion", but why does he add the word "forbearance"? Maybe he has been inspired by some Chinese *kungfu* movies produced in Taiwan and Hong Kong. In many of such movies, factions of martial arts often put up a Chinese character "*ren*" (forbearance) in a large size and take it as a discipline of disciples; possibly because the worst thing for people skillful at martial arts is impulsion, they especially have to tolerate others! Moreover, in some *kungfu* movies, the "*renzhe*" (忍者ninja) from Japan are very skillful in martial arts and are even able to come and go like a shadow. So, it is also possible that Li has been inspired by the Japanese. For the practice of the way of Bodhisattvas in Buddhism, there are six cardinal kinds of guidance (六波羅蜜多six kinds of perfection [paramita]), which are namely donation, the abidance by disciplines, the tolerance of shame, diligence, sustained concentration and wisdom. In particular, the 3rd one "the tolerance of shame" is also called "the Perfection of Patience (Kshanti Paramita)", which is a profound kind of self-restraint, but it is merely one of the six cardinal kinds of guidance. If Li's "forbearance" sources from this idea, it cannot be considered as consummate, either.

4. As for the two words "truthfulness" and "compassion", possibly Li Hongzhi has misunderstood them too. The cultivation of "truthfulness" in Daojiao道教 sourced from the thought of "returning to simplicity and truth" of Daojia道家 ,⑥ but Laotze and Zhuangzi's returning to "truth" means the return to the nature or naturalness,

which is the opposition to all artificial things in the human society, including such regulations as rites and laws. Li Hongzhi repeatedly stresses that all in the universe has been predestined, alleging that "naturalness does not exist",⑦ does he not contradict himself when he borrows the word "*zhen*" (truth or truthfulness) from Daojia (an academic school represented by Laotze and Zhuangzi and embracing the Tao, different from the Daojiao as a religion) as the spiritual standard of "Falun Gong"?! Moreover, it is true that Buddhism talks "compassion", but it does not lay an emphasis on "*shan*" (good or compassion); instead, it is focused on the "emancipation" from afflictions. As for this point, we can take the Chan School as evidence. The Chan School holds that a person "can realize his original mind only when his mind does not cling to good or evil" (The *Platform Sutra*壇經 says, "Not thinking of good, and not thinking of evil. Only at that moment it is the original appearance). So, it can be seen that the emphasis of Buddhism is the "surpassing of *shan* (good)". At this point Li Hongzhi obviously misunderstands it once again.

5. Judging from the point of practice, the authenticity of "Truthfulness, Compassion and Forbearance" that Li has paraded is suspicious, too. He plagiarizes a muddle of terms from Buddhism, Taoism and sciences and alleges them to be the "cosmic law" that has never been revealed in the past thousands of millions of years. Is it a "truth"? Over these ten years, Li Hongzhi has stayed in exile in the USA, but he constantly instigates his disciples in the mainland to wage political struggles in the name of "true dharma", it is not different from "pushing disciples up to the battle lines and letting them join the fight with tigers for their master". Can it be called "*shan*" (good or compassion)? As for "forbearance", the above quoted

have shown his contradiction. In addition, his freak reason even contains more self-contradiction: Now that "forbearance" is an attribute of the universe, it should have its consistency; why does it suddenly become "beyond endurance", the opposition of "forbearance" at certain levels? This cannot happen unless it loses its consistency. But once it loses its consistency, it cannot be the "quality of the universe" anymore; rather, it should have been the "randomicity".

Overall, no matter whether as "the ultimate principle of the universe"⑧ or "spiritual standard", "Truthfulness, Compassion and Forbearance" are all untenable. With respect to Li's behaviors in reality, it is also questionable whether they comply with these three words.

Notes:
1. For the five passages quoted above, see the *Zhuan Falun*, pp. 15-18.
2. Ibid, p. 45.
3. The *Falun Fofa—Essentials for Further Advances*, p. 74.
4. Ibid, p. 41.
5. For the details of "four immeasurable minds", see the author's *Selection of Buddhist Doctrines*, Chapter 6, Section 5, Item 4.
6. "Daojia"（道家） and "Daojiao" （道教）are different terms; the former refers to the thoughts of Laotze and Zhuangzi, whereas the latter suggests various sects among folks established since Zhang Daoling張道陵 (A. D. 34-156?) of the late Han Dynasty. Li does not know the difference.
7. See the *Falun Fofa—Essentials for Further Advances*, p.123.

8. In recent years, Professor Wu Rujun(吳汝鈞) has synthesized both Eastern and Western philosophical thoughts and religious doctrines, proposing the "phenomenology of pure vitality" as the ultimate principle of the universe. This theory is unprecedented; those who are interested in profound philosophical research may have an eye on it. See Professor Wu, the *Phenomenology of Pure Vitality* (纯粹力動現象學) and its sequence, Taiwan Commercial Press, 2005 & 2008.

The Nonsense about "Reality-bodies"

What is closely related to "Falun" is Li Hongzhi's nonsense about "reality-bodies". Or one can say that the whole "theoretical foundation" of "Falun Gong" is based on this nonsense. So long as the nonsense about "reality-bodies" is refuted, the whole "Dafa" (theory) will collapse.

The Meaning of Reality-body

Reality-body（法身） is a unique term of Buddhism, and it originally refers to the spiritual aspect of Sakyamuni.

When Sakyamuni (the Buddha) stayed in this world, he instructed his disciples all his life, and lived together with them; it was quite like the living style of Confucius in China. The disciples respected their master very much, but they merely viewed him as a senior with great personality and considerable knowledge, and did not consecrate him as a God or superman yet. Hundreds of years later after the Buddha's passing, the disciples of later generations gradually apotheosized him and worshiped him as a God for the sake of requirement in the spread of their doctrines. Hence there emerged the theory that the Buddha has "two forms of bodies" or "three forms of bodies".

The "theory of two forms of bodies" means that in addition to his physical body (body of flesh and blood as that of an ordinary human being), the Buddha has also a "reality-body", which refers to a spiritual thing-in-itself.

Later on, the "theory of two forms of bodies" developed into the "theory of three forms of bodies". This new theory argues that the Buddha has three forms of bodies: reality-body, reward body and transformation-response bodies. The names of the "three forms of bodies" vary because of the difference of sects, for example, they are respectively called "reality-body", "transformation-response bodies" and "transformation bodies" in some sects. Comprehensively, the term of "three forms of bodies" further developed, and thus emerged the theory of "four forms of bodies" (reality-body, reward body, transformation-response bodies and transformation bodies). Li Hongzhi's profession of "four forms of bodies" in a poem quoted above in the 3rd section titled "Li Hongzhi's Works" just alludes to the final form of theory of its kind.

No matter however it developed, however, "reality-body" refers to the truth that the Buddha had verified and demonstrated; such truth is prevalent all over the whole universe, that is, it (the truth) exists throughout the One Billion Worlds. The "reward body" is a body as a reward obtained due to the "reality-body"; the Mahavairocana Buddha enshrined in some Buddhist temples is just "the Buddha with a reward body", who signifies a universal blaze of light. The "transformation-response bodies" (or transformation bodies) means the bodies of flesh and blood in which the Buddha incarnated himself in response to the requirement of living beings in the world, for example, Sakyamuni was just a "Buddha with a transformation-response body" when he lived in the world.

Such complicated theory was not completely produced by the Mahayana Consciousness-only School four hundred years later after the passing of the Buddha. This sect argues that the "three forms of bodies" contain three elements: self-nature body (dharmakaya), enjoyment-body (samboghakaya) and transformation body (nirmana-kaya). The self-nature body is just the "reality-body", which stands for the form of principles as the true-thusness that the Thus-Come obtained through the verification and demonstration by himself, or the invisible, transcendent and abstract principle of the universe.

It belongs to the world of "things-in-itself". When this principle is concretely embodied in the world, it is just the "enjoyment-body" (reward body) and "transformation body".①

The above is merely a brief introduction to the source and meaning of "reality-body" . Now, let's come back to appreciate how Li talks nonsense.

Li Hongzhi's Reality-bodies

In Li Hongzhi's book, readers can find everywhere his profession of his "reality-bodies", and his "reality-bodies" are peerlessly powerful, much more powerful than that of the Thus-Come Buddha; it sounds like a fairy tale or sleep-talking. The quotations below are some of his original texts.

> *"Because I have numberless reality-bodies, which have my very powerful supernatural force; they can show very powerful supernatural force, very powerful force based on Dharma."*②

Surprisingly he professes to "have numberless reality-bodies" and "very powerful supernatural force"! Could he prove it to people?

> *"My reality-bodies are surely to protect you until you can protect yourselves; by then you will have completed your practice of the worldly dharma, and you will have obtained the Way."*③

> *"It is really too difficult for an individual to practice; without the protection provided by my reality-bodies, you cannot practice at all. You may be involved into the fatal problems immediately after you leave home."*④

> *"When you spread the Gong, some of you may think like this: The master is able to embed falun and adjust physical conditions for trainees, but what can we do since we are not able to do that ourselves? It does not matter. As I've told you, behind each trainee there is a reality-body of mine, and they are more than one, so my reality-bodies will do such things."*⑤

That is why the "disciples" must believe in, rely on and esteem "Master Li Hongzhi"! It reminds people of the maxim "Faith, Hope and Love" often hung on the exterior wall of Christian churches.

"A man will be able to produce a reality-body when he elevates himself above a certain level beyond the transmundane dharma through practice. The reality-body is generated at the place of dantian of a human being; it is composed both Fa and Gong, and is manifested in another space. A reality-body has its very powerful prowess, but its consciousness and thoughts are controlled by the main body. On the other hand, a reality-body itself is complete, independent, real and individual life, so it itself is able to do anything. A reality-body does things exactly the same as the main consciousness of a person wants to, exactly the same. That matter will be done that way if it is done by the human being himself, and it will be done that way too if it is done by a reality-body; that is what we mean by reality-bodies. When I want to do something, for example, to adjust the body of a disciple who is really practicing, I do it through my reality-bodies...A reality-body does not have the body of an ordinary human being, and it is represented in another space. That form of life is not fixed or unchangeable; it can become larger or smaller. Sometimes it becomes very large, so large that one cannot have an entire sight of its head; and sometimes it becomes very small, so small that it is even smaller than cells."⑥

Surprisingly, "reality-bodies" have been produced from nearby a navel (*dantian*). It can become larger and smaller, and even smaller than cells! So, it seems to be more powerful than the 72 changes of Sun Wukong (孫悟空Monkey King) in *The Journey to the West* (西遊記).

"Reality-bodies are just the representation of my omnipresent wisdom, and they are not independent life...Falun is also another representation form of the characteristics of my

supernatural force and Dafa wisdom, and is indescribably wonderful. Falun is the representation of dharma-nature in all materials from macro to micro in the universe, and also it is not independent life."

"Reality-bodies cannot be cognized the same way as the concept of completely independent life, and the reason is that they are just the satisfactory representation of a primary body's image, spiritual force, dharma prowess and wisdom. They have the ability to independently do anything in the light of the will of a primary body...Actually, in plain words, my reality-bodies are just me myself." ⑦

Through all these tortuous talks, Li Hongzhi finally speaks the truth out: "In plain words, my reality-bodies are just me myself." It is more than the promotion of superstition--It is essentially the serious superstition about himself.

"Those who have not been enlightened pay attention to this! Those who have not been enlightened can also have reality-bodies if they cultivate themselves up to the level of the Buddha, but none of our present trainees, including the qigong masters of other qigong factions today, has reached such a realm. So far as I know, I am the only one who has reality-bodies." ⑧

Li's "obduracy to self" is so intense that we cannot but suspect that he is really insane. In the light of the Consciousness-only Theory of Buddhism, this is a serious "wrong views". ⑨

Absurd Logic

Li Hongzhi always speaks of "reality-bodies" whenever he talks, and he has many writings about "reality-bodies", but the quotation above must have been enough to remind readers of the "comedic" language in the popular movies and TV shows in Hong Kong and Taiwan in recent 30 years.

To sum up the sections and related remarks above, Li Hongzhi's absurd logic about "reality-bodies" can be generalized as the following six points:

1. Why do people want to practice "Falun Gong"? Because they can obtain reality-bodies after they practice it, they would have supernatural abilities and would even be able to "have an eternal original spirit" (元神不滅) after they obtain reality-bodies.

2. Why are people able to practice? It is because there is a "*falun*" permanently turning in each of their abdomens.

3. Why do they have a "*falun*" in their lower abdomens? It is because Li Hongzhi has embedded them for everyone.

4. How can Li Hongzhi alone embed "*falun*" in the *dantian* of more than a hundred million disciples as he has claimed? It is because Li has numerous "reality-bodies", and thus is able to control things in any places at any time.

5. How can a person manage to receive a "*falun*" from Li Hongzhi? You can do it merely by reading his "scriptures" or watching his "*hong fa*"(洪法) (Li Hongzhi's dharma) video tapes.

6. Why does Li Hongzhi have such great supernatural force? Because he is not an ordinary man, instead, he comes from the highest level of spaces in the universe, and much powerful than Laotze, the Buddha and Jesus.

Obviously, Li Hongzhi does not know what "reality-bodies" means in Buddhism, he is simply using this term to talk nonsense, making it a sharp weapon to control the minds of others. It is rather immoral.

If Li Hongzhi does not agree with the above refutation and analysis, he can provide pertinent evidence to prove he himself does have such powerful "reality-bodies" now that he is a man fond of "science". We must be aware that science is particular about demonstration (see the details of the principle of demonstration in the section below). In the opinion of the author, the most powerful evidence at present is nothing but turning the CPC Central Committee's decision to ban "Falun Gong" into a decision to commend "the great contributions made by Li Hongzhi". If he could do so, the author would be convinced that all the believers of all the other religions in the world, including Protestantism, Catholicism, Islam, Buddhism, Hinduism, Taoism and so on, would have been converted to Li's "Falun Dafa". So, Master Li, perform your "high energy of reality-bodies" soon!

Notes:

1. As for these theories about "the bodies of the Buddha", see Wu Rujun, *Concepts and Philosophical Methods in Buddhism*, (吳汝鈞: 佛教的概念與方法) p. 19, Taiwan Commercial Press, 1992.
2. *Zhuan Falun*, p. 150.
3. Ibid, p. 153.
4. Ibid, p. 252.
5. Ibid, p. 159.
6. Ibid, p. 222.
7. *Essentials for Further Advances*, pp. 72 & 77.
8. *Falun Dafa Interpretation*, p. 199.
9. According to the Consciousness-only Theory (唯識論) in Buddhism, "wrong views" are one of the six fundamental kinds of afflictions, and it can be sub-divided into five kinds:

   1) Self view: Also known as satkaya or the view of the existence of a self. It means the intense insistency on self, for example, stubbornly claiming that one has eternal soul,

yuan shen (original spirit) and reality-body in one's conceit.

2) Extreme view: It either holds that all is true (eternalism) or that all is nothingness. Actually, both are wrong.

3) Evil view: This view holds that there are no causes or results, and that there is no difference between committing evils and performing charitable deeds.

4) View of attachment to views: The clinging to certain wrong view or theory (ideology). For example, as Li Hongzhi keeps stressing his "Dafa" in the face of his disciples, some people who have poor discretion will be gradually convinced by him, and thus form the view of attachment to views. And so it is with Li himself, and it is called "negative self psychological suggestion" in modern psychology (see Section 23 infra titled "Magic Use of Nouns".

5) View of rigid attachment to the precepts: Clinging to certain evil precepts and turning it into foolish deeds. See the author's *Selection of Buddhist Doctrines*, Chapter Three, Section Three, One Hundred Dharma.

The Myth of "Science"

For recent two hundred years, science and technology have rapidly advanced. Everyone has come into contact with the achievements of science and technology and personally experienced the benefits that they have brought about no matter whether in the fields of physics, chemistry, medicine, outer space or the sphere of daily life. Consequently, people have thus formed such opinions as that "science is omnipotent", that "science is just the truth" and that "science is objective". These opinions are called "scientism" in philosophy.

Man is a rational animal, while scientific knowledge is just the result of rationality, so scientific knowledge is important and valuable. But man's spiritual functions are extremely complicated, besides rationality, there are at least feelings, will, the sense of morality and the pursuit of metaphysical principles. So, in addition to scientific knowledge, there are also literature, music, fine arts and so on based on feelings, let alone ethics and moral norms ruling common social life, and religious beliefs transcending the reality and pursuing ultimate meanings. Therefore, it is right for man to give a play to the rationality of science, but it is wrong to embrace "scientism" and even "pseudoscience" by doing everything under the banner of "science".

Li Hongzhi Muddles Beliefs with Science

What is the nature of "Falun Gong"? To put it bluntly, it is that Li Hongzhi hopes to establish a "new religion" which takes himself as the hierarch and even "the only true god" (He calls himself "master", and such a "master" is one and the only). In order to pander to the tide of times, he constantly fiddles with scientific terms, wishing to win people's trust and support. In this way, however, he has unconsciously trapped himself into "scientism" without knowing it. Anyone of insight knows that all religious sects under the banner of "science" since the early modern times have been absurd and even deceptive; for since Immanuel Kant (1724—1804), intelligentsia has recognized that belief and science are two different things, and it is absurd to lump these two together.①

Li Hongzhi frequently resorts to science and tries to prove his theory with some scientific terms when he promotes his "Fofa". For example, he says,

> *"Fofa is the insight into all mysteries, ranging from things as small as particles and molecules to things as large as the universe, and it is all-embracing, leaving nothing unincluded...Fofa is the only one that has completely disclosed the mysteries of the universe, time and space, and human bodies...And Fofa is the only one that has made clear the mysteries of each space of man, substantial existences, life and the whole universe."②*

This is completely muddling "belief" with "science". If Li Hongzhi's "Fofa" could really reveal the "mysteries of the universe, time and space, and human bodies", all the departments and institutes of natural sciences in all colleges and universities all over the world could have been closed, and Li himself should have been more than due for the Nobel prizes in physics, chemistry and peace.

The Judgment Criteria of Science

Science values practical test and verification, which are called "demonstration". There are three principles that must be followed:

1. Repeatability: The results of test and verification must be "time-tested". For example, suppose a certain kind of drug is said to have a dormitive effects; after many times of tests it is proved to be so, then that can be considered as scientific knowledge. Another example is the theory about radio waves. People thus invented radiotelegraphy, listen to radio broadcast and watch satellite TV and so on, this proves that it is true, so it is scientific knowledge.

2. Commonality: Anyone can get the same result so long as he tests it in the light of certain procedures. For example, under normal air pressure, liquid water becomes gas when it is heated up to 100°C, and freezes when the temperature is lowered to 0°C. This is a certain result that everyone can get so long as he does the experiment. For another example, the sum of three interior angles of a triangle is 180°, anyone will get the same result if he measures it (Math is the very foundation of science, so science can be deduced from math).

3. Falsifiability: Scientific knowledge does not guarantee that it itself is not always absolutely right on any occasion; after the knowledge level of man is improved, it can deny previous wrong knowledge. For example, after Albert Einstein's "view on time and space" (general relativity theory) came into being, the view that "time and space are not related" in the times of Isaac Newton appears obviously wrong in the macro cosmology. Therefore, science does not proclaim what is "absolute truth that never changes" anymore.

A religious belief does not comply with any
of the above-mentioned three principles.

With respect to the first and the second principles, belief does not comply with any of them. For example, some people profess that they see certain revelation that Jesus gives them in their prayers; even if those people feel such "miracles" are true, they are merely their personal experiences, which have no "repeatability" (not that they can repeatedly see them again if they want) or "communality" (others who want to see Jesus cannot see him), therefore, beliefs are not science.

With regard to the third principle, beliefs have nothing to do with falsifiability. For example, as for the matter of ghosts and gods, you cannot "prove" their existence, nor can you "prove" their non-existence; any attempt to make such "proof" belongs to absurdity. The matter of beliefs is often beyond the intellectuality of man (for example, ghosts and gods cannot be taken as the targets of our knowledge); people attempt in vain to "prove" or "falsify" such things as ghosts and gods only when they are not aware of the limitation of man's cognitive ability. So, what is it if it is not absurdity?

That was why Confucius refused to answer his disciple's question when the latter asked whether there were ghosts or gods after the deaths of human beings. (論語・先進Xianjin in *The Analects of Confucius* says, "Jilu asked about how to serve ghosts and gods, the Master replied, "How could you serve ghosts before you are able to serve human beings?" then, Jilu asked about death, and the Master answered in a similar way, "How could you know death before you know life?") The very reason that a saint was a saint was that he did not try to "prove" or "falsify" the matter of ghosts or gods. And that is why Confucius said that "To acknowledge what is known as known and what is not known as not known is knowledge." (Weizheng為政, *The Analects of Confucius*)

Science is based on "demonstration", and the above-mentioned is the brief principle of "demonstration". If Li Hongzhi's "Dafa" really comply with "science" so much, he must provide some "demonstration", or otherwise he would be talking nonsense or deceiving.

The Logic to Cognize Truth

The issue of "separation of science from religious beliefs" is both important and profound, and cannot be easily understood by the multitude, so "pseudoscience" is often able to prevail. Here, the author would like to take this occasion to discuss it by the profound teachings of Buddhism, and hope it help people of all circles easily grasp this issue.

In An Examination of Self and Phenomena, a chapter in the *Madhyamika-sastra* (中論 • 觀法品) by Nagarjuna, there is a verse which says that *"All reality is non-reality, it is reality and meanwhile non-reality; it is non-reality and meanwhile not non-reality, and that is what all Dharma is."* This is famous "four-sentence logic", a unique Buddhist means to cognize the reality. Now, let's analyze the general meanings of this verse:

> *The first sentence: All things are "real".*
> *The second sentence: Nothing is really "real".*
> *The third sentence: All is "real" and nothing is really "real" on the other hand.*
> *The fourth sentence: Nothing is really "real", but at the same time nothing is really "unreal".*

As for the cognition of all things in the world, some are true (real), and some others are false (unreal); this is the cognition of an ordinary person, and also it is the very basis of science. This is the logic contained in the first and the second sentences. While the "real" and "false" are further combined, it is dialectics. This is the third sentence. While both the "real" and the "false" are surpassed, it is the most advanced logic of Buddhism . This is the fourth sentence (i.e., non-duality dharma-gate, see details in the section below).

If in the terms of the western modern symbolic logic, these four sentences can be expressed as follows:

The first sentence is an affirmative proposition: P

The second sentence is a negative proposition: $\sim P$

The third sentence is a combination
of the first and the second sentences: $P \cdot \sim P$

The fourth sentence is the negation
of the third sentence: $\sim (P \cdot \sim P)$

In order to make such logic more easily understood, let's represent truth (reality) with A, and falseness (non-reality) with B, then we have the following four formulae:

1. A
2. B
3. A + B
4. − (A + B)

From the point of view of Nagarjuna's four sentence logic of truth, we can know that all secular knowledge (worldly truths), including scientific knowledge, is at the level of truth and falseness. But what is "true" and what is "false"? It has to be tested through facts. While one is able to further realize that truth contains falseness and vice versa, just as the Confucianism and Taoism of China have always taught, "mishaps and blessings are interdependent", i.e. while one can look at things by combining both A and B, he will have reached the level of "dialectic logic" in F. Hegel's term, that is, the "dialectics" that some modern politicians often mention. In comparison, the highest teaching of Buddhism (ultimate truth) surpasses (A+B).

Nagarjuna's "four-sentence logic"③ can help us understand more deeply that science and belief are two different things: science is formal knowledge that must be based on demonstration, while the most profound teachings of a religion cannot be grasped without tacit realization. "Explicit understanding" and "tacit realization" are different, of course. Li Hongzhi confuses science with religion, so people cannot help but suspecting he not only knows nothing about Buddhism, but also knows nothing about science: he is merely muddling some scientific nouns frequently seen in newspapers and journals and stretching their meanings, thinking that he would be able to deceive people in this way.

What Is Matter?

What is more absurd is Li's idea about "matter":

*"Now, people have found elements such as infrasonic waves, ultrasonic waves, electromagnetic waves, infrared, gamma rays, neutrons, atoms and trace elements with instruments on qigong masters. Are these not matter? They are also matter. Is anything not composed of matter?"*④

*"What is xin-xing (心性mind and nature)? xin-xing include morality (morality is a kind of matter)…Any matter in the universe, including all the matter pervading in the universe, is in the form of spirituality, they all have their minds, and are all the forms of existence of cosmic law at different levels."*⑤

*"There is a field around a human body. This field is just morality we usually talk about. Morality is a kind of white material, it is not a thing of spirituality of human beings as we used to imagine, things in the consciousness of man are completely a kind of existence as matter…There is also a kind of black matter which exists at the same time, we call it yeli (業力the force of intention and activity, or the function or effect of karma)… Both white matter and black matter exist simultaneously."*⑥

It is already questionable to call sound waves, electromagnetic waves, neutrons, infrared and so on the "matter" in a physical sense, now he calls morality, karma and even man's spirit and consciousness "matter". Evidently Li has no scientific knowledge such as physics.

Then, what is "matter"? This has been a question ceaselessly debated in the western philosophy ever since the ancient Greece 2,500 years ago. By the early modern times, J. Locke (1632-1704), an important British philosopher, proposed his theory about the "primary qualities" and "secondary qualities" of matter, which becomes a recognized standard among later generations.⑦ After the emergence of modern "quantum theory" and "phenomenology", however, Locke's theory about matter has been questioned. No matter how it develops, however, there are two points that should be stressed:

1. Only things that have the "quality of extension" (i.e., the occupation of space) are called "matter" (that is the most basic "primary quality" of matter), or otherwise they cannot be viewed as "matter", for example, sound waves, gravitation, magnetic fields and so forth are not matter because they do not occupy any spaces.

2. At all times and in all countries, there is no theory that calls "spiritual functions" (for examples, the effects of karma in Buddhism, moralities, the power of will, emotions and so forth) "matter". Exactly on the contrary, "spirit" is the opposite noun of "matter", and these two absolutely cannot be viewed the same.

Obviously, Li Hongzhi says so because he does not understand the word "matter". With respect to such refutation and analysis, probably he would rebuke as such, "The matter I talk about is not the concept of your common science, what I speak of is the cosmic law, which is beyond you mediocre people's understanding!" Li has employed such a method in many questionable issues. Actually it is the worst sophistry, a logical contradiction (While he employs the scientific noun "matter", he denies this noun with a non-scientific reason. This is a breach of the law of contradiction. So, his reasoning is false). This is really an anti-intellectual act which aims at deception. If the theory about "evil karma" is true, he himself has committed serious evil karma.⑧

The Myth of Dafa

Li Hongzhi even professes that he is able to check out the history of evolution of the universe and mankind:

> *"In the immense universe, in the movement of the Galaxy, the motions of our earth cannot be smooth all the time; probably it would crash into another star, or there emerged other problems which had caused dreadful disasters. From the point of view of our Gong, that is how things have been designed. Once upon a time, I carefully checked it. As a result, I found mankind had been in the state of extinction for 81 times, only a few survived, with a little pre-history cultivation left; the survivors entered the next period, living a primitive life. Afterwards, the*

*population of mankind grew, and civilization emerged at last once again. After 81 periodic changes as such, still I have not seen its end."*⑨

How did Li Hongzhi "find out" that mankind has experienced 81 disasters? Could he have been inspired by the story of Tang-Monk's（唐僧） 81 mischances in the *Journey to the West*? If he could really show some "proof of his verification", he must have been able to be awarded with a Nobel prize in physics. If he cannot show any proof, he would have been simply weaving his "myth of Dafa" with scientific nouns.

Li's "works" are full of such "myths". Actually, it is acceptable to Buddhism to invent a new belief so long as it is beneficial to others, for Buddhism would view it as one of "expedient means". But as the myths become two absurd, possibly they cannot be viewed as a belief, but a joke only.

Notes:
1. Immanuel Kant was one of the most important philosophers in the West in the early modern times. He tried to reason whether "god" or "soul" exist, only to find some "antinomies", that is, the rational knowledge of us as human beings are unable to verify whether these two exist or not. But in "practical reason" (morality, beliefs, and so forth), gods or souls should be admitted. This theory is influential to the thoughts of later generations; at present, the circle of philosophy has recognized that science and belief are things in two different fields in the mind of human beings, that these two cannot be unified, and that one cannot be equated with the other.
2. *Zhuan Falun*, pp. 1-2.
3. For the detail of this four-sentence logic, see Wu Rujun, *Philosophical Interpretation of Nagarjuna'*

Madhyamika-sastra（龍樹中論的哲學解讀）, p. 327 and infra. Taiwan Commercial Press, 1999, 3rd print run.

4. *Zhuan Falun*, p. 27.
5. Ibid, pp. 30-31.
6. Ibid, pp. 35-36.
7. Locke held that matter has both main primary and secondary qualities. The former are ontological qualities such as "extension" (the occupation of space), "motions and stillness" and "numbers", while the latter such as color, sound, fragrance, taste and so forth are attributes that must be perceived through man's sense organs. Therefore, the "primary qualities" are the nature of matter, but the "secondary qualities" are about the sense organs and thoughts of man. This equates to viewing "matter" as the primary qualities, while "spirit" as secondary. This theory has exerted great influence over physics and some social philosophy afterwards. As for Locke's theories, see Bertrand Russell, *A History of Western Philosophy*, p. 677, the version of Qiu Yanxi's translation, Taiwan Zhonghua Book Company.
8. The term "karma" in Buddhism involves very profound classics, here the author is not going to expatiate on it, but what is sure is that Li has talked it completely wrongly. Those who are interested can consult Li Runsheng's *Interpretations of Karmasiddhi-prakara!a*（李潤生：大乘成業論釋義）, Taipei BuddhAll Cultural Enterprise Co., Ltd. This book has expatiated on the issue of "karma".
9. *Zhuan Falun*, p. 23.

What Is "Bu Er Fa Men"?

"Bu er fa men" (不二法門 actually meaning "non-duality dharma-gate", but misunderstood by Li Hongzhi as "no other gate to the dharma") is a frequent expression in Li Hongzhi's writings, but he does not understand the true meaning of this Buddhist term at all; instead, he simply takes the words too literally, and becomes the laughingstock of insightful people.

He frequently stresses that the practitioners of his Falun Gong must be wholehearted, and it absolutely cannot be mixed with any other things, no matter whether they are *qigong*, Taoism or Buddhism. Or otherwise, you would "go wrong", "run into troubles" and "lose your minds", consequently his "reality-bodies" would not take care of you anymore, and you would not be able to obtain any "Fa".①

To stress this point, he often takes the Buddhist expression "non-duality dharma-gate" as circumstantial evidence, saying that Buddhism also stresses *"bu er fa men"*—A practitioner is allowed to intently practice one single dharma-gate, and cannot simultaneously practice any other dharma-gate. Now, let's quote a paragraph from his writings as evidence:

> *"We must be intent when we practice. No matter how you practice, you cannot mix it with anything in the past. Some laymen practice both Buddhism and our Falun Gong. Let me*

tell you, you will get nothing at the end, and nobody will give you anything. We all belong to Buddhism, but here is a question of mind and nature, and meanwhile a question of intentness. You have only one single body, what kind of gong (the effect gained through the practice of Gong) would be generated in your bodies? How to evolve for you? Where are you going? Which dharma-gate you choose, you will go where it leads you to…This is just as religion has mentioned, it is called non-duality dharma-gate…Not only that the practice of Gong and the cultivation of Buddhists in temples cannot be muddled up, but also that different methods of practice, different qigong and different religions shall not be mixed together. Even in the same religion, different dharma-gate cannot be mixed together; instead, you can choose only one single dharma-gate. For example, if you choose to practice the Pure Land, then just cling to the Pure Land; if you choose to practice Esoteric Buddhism, then just cling to Esoteric Buddhism; if you choose to practice the Chan School, then just cling to the Chan School. If you run after two hares at the same time, practicing both this and that, you will get nothing at the end. In other words, even Buddhism has stressed bu er fa men, not allowing you mix miscellaneous dharma-gates to practice."②

In this paragraph, Li said that "even Buddhism has stressed 'bu er fa men', not allowing you mix miscellaneous dharma-gate to practice." That is nonsense due to his total ignorance of the Buddhist expression "*bu er fa men*" (non-duality dharma-gate). Moreover, he does not know that Buddhism has been encouraging its believers to simultaneously practice several dharma-gates. He has explained it exactly the other way round!

The Meaning of "Bu Er Fa Men"

The Buddhist expression "*bu er fa men*" (不二法门 non-duality dharma-gate) is a very profound concept, which common people cannot easily understand. But "*bu er fa men*" absolutely does not mean that a practitioner "can practice only one dharma-gate, and shall not be between two stools" as Li Hongzhi has mentioned. The reason is that it does not mean a practitioner "shall not practice two dharma-gates"; instead, it means "the gate of 'non-duality dharma'". Then, what is "the gate of 'non-duality dharma'"? The expression "non-duality dharma" suggests an absolute realm, and the word "gate" means "way" or "path". Now, let's briefly explain it as follows.

Man's cognition of things is based on the view (category) of "duality", for example, high and low, big and small, good and bad, good and evil, true and false, many and few, come and go, life and death, and so forth. In a relation of duality, two views have the quality of "relativity", that is, the two have their meanings only when they depend upon each other. Without "big", there would be no "small", and vice versa. Now that it is "relativity", it is not "absoluteness"; so, the so-called "non-duality dharma" just means to transcend the relativity of duality and reach the realm of absoluteness.

Moreover, from the point of view of the four-sentence verse in Nagarjuna's *Madhyamika-sastra*, the "reality" in the first sentence and the "non-reality" in the second one are exactly two relative concept, that is, "dharma of duality"; the "reality and meanwhile the non-reality" in the third sentence is the integration of the dharma of duality, and the "non-reality and meanwhile not the non-duality" in the fourth sentence has surpassed the realm of "dharma of duality", that is, it has reached the realm of absoluteness.

In order to suit for different people, times and sites, Buddhism advocates all kinds of convenient dharma-gate to learn and practice Buddhism. For example, Chinese believers like to go to Buddhist temples to worship the Buddha by incensing; actually, Buddhism did not intend to endorse the worship of clay idols, let alone the presentation of incense. Only because the Chinese believers have formed such customs and habits, Buddhism does not exclude it; instead, it views such activities as a "dharma-gate" for the convenience of the Chinese people. As the most tolerate religion, Buddhism allows any "dharma-gate" that is conducive to relieving the sufferings of living beings. So, there goes the saying of "Eighty-four thousand dharma-gates" in Buddhism. Here, the number "eighty-four thousand" was simply a parlance that the ancient Indians used to mean "many" or "numerousness", which is like the "*Qianqian Wanwan*" (千千萬萬 hundreds of thousands) in Chinese, and it does not refer to any definite number. In a word, the expression "Eighty-four thousand dharma-gates" means numerous dharma-gates, this must be kept in mind; and more importantly, Buddhism encourages the practice of multiple dharma-gates, this must be kept in mind, too.

Then, what does "*bu er fa men*" means? It does not mean that a practitioner can choose only one among the "eighty-four thousand dharma-gates"; instead, it means "the gate of non-duality dharma". In other words, it is also a dharma-gate, only that it is the dharma-gate at the highest level, a dharma-gate that surpasses all the other "dharma-gates".

Non-duality Dharma-gate Is Just the Dharma of Reality

The highest "gate of dharma" that surpasses all the other dharma-gates is just the absolute realm that has surmounted duality, that is, the "dharma of reality". As the Buddhist sutras say, "Real appearances have no appearances, and they are just the Thusness." This sentence means that the highest thing-in-itself (Here the author expediently calls it "thing-in-itself" so that the common readers can easily understand it; in fact, Buddhism promotes "emptiness" and denies any "thing-in-itself", and in Buddhist sutras it is often called the True-thusness, real appearances, reality, just-as-it-is-ness and so on) is unimaginably beyond the cognitive reason of human beings, and is a realm that can be known only through "tacit realization".

As for the above-mentioned, a famous Buddhist sutra titled "*Vimalakirti Sutra*" (维摩經) has explained it most wonderfully; here, let's introduce a little about it and take it as a piece of evidence for the refutation and analysis.

The main points of this sutra are as follows: Vimalakirti was a great layman in the Vaishali Town, who had considerable knowledge, great wisdom and extraordinary achievements in practicing Buddhism, and had been highly respected by Sakyamuni. The Buddha often asked Vimalakirti to instruct his disciples instead when he was not convenient to teach them sometimes.

Once upon a time, the great layman felt uncomfortable, so the Buddha sent Manjusri（文殊菩薩） to head a large group of other disciples who had made considerable achievements in practicing Buddhism to show his solicitude, but actually, the Buddha intended the great layman to instruct his disciples. After they wished the great layman good health, the disciples stayed nearby to listen to the great layman and Manjusri talking about some profound Buddhist doctrines, and each of them were greatly benefited.

And then the scripture climaxed with this: Vimalakirti asked the others a most profound question, "What is called to enter 'non-duality dharma-gate'?" and he asked everyone in the presence gave their answers as they liked. After 30 bodhisattvas gave their answers one by one, the greatly layman directly asked Bodhisattva Manjusri to express his opinion. Manjusri replied,

"As for all dharma, one says nothing, expresses nothing, knows nothing, and keeps away from questions and answers; that is the entrance of the non-duality dharma-gate."

(This passage means that the research of things has transcended phenomena and reached the realm of Reality; such a realm is beyond language and knowledge, and cannot be discussed in the pattern of questions and answers. In this way, one can enter the "gate of non-duality dharma")

And then, Manjusri asked Vimalakirti in turn, which introduced a wonderful passage:

*"We have expressed our opinions each, will you the Master tell us what a bodhisattva's entrance into the gate of non-duality dharma-gate is, please?" At these words, Vimalakirti remained tacit. Then, Manjusri exclaimed, "Marvelous! Really Marvelous! He is so brilliant that he has abandoned any language; this is really the entrance of the gate of non-duality dharma."*③

This is the very famous principle of "the great sage's reticence" (聖默然). Bodhisattva Manjusri had expressed that "only the transcendence over words and languages is the entrance into the gate of non-duality dharma", his so-called "non-language" was still expressed through language, so only Vimalakirti' tacitness is the true "non-language of non-language", the highest expressive pattern. That is why Manjusri exclaimed. Such a realm of abstruse principle is often described with two sentences in Buddhist scriptures: "The path of language is cut off, and the ubiety of mental formations vanishes." (言語道斷，心行處滅) —Such a realm is quite beyond any language or thinking.

The *Vimalakirti Sutra* was translated by Kumarajiva (鳩摩羅什), and was annotated by Kumarajiva himself and his outstanding disciple Monk Zhao(僧肇). Now let's quote the two persons' explanations about "non-duality dharma", which should be helpful for readers to further understand this abstruse question.

> *"Kumarajiva said, 'The dependent origination of existence is based on duality dharma. Once duality dharma is abandoned, there will be the realm of abstruseness.'"*

The passage above can be paraphrased as such: Kumarajiva said that all the existences in the world must be based on opposite concepts which are two poles (for examples, "being" and "non-being", "many" and "few", "love" and "hatred", "upper" and "lower", "front" and "back"... These are all duality dharma, i.e., two poles—opposite concepts). If we erase the concepts of opposition from our minds, we immediately enter the realm of abstruseness and wonder.

Monk Zhao further explained:

> *" Any deviation from the Truth is called duality, so we speak of non-duality.'"*

> *"The so-called non-duality means no difference, and it just alludes to the oneness and reality mentioned in scriptures. The principle of oneness and reality is characterized with abstruseness*

and stillness, free from phenomena; it stresses just-as-it-is-ness and equality, and denies any difference between this and that. That is why it is described as non-duality."

The two passages can be paraphrased as follows: What does non-duality mean? It means "no difference", and the so-called "oneness and reality" in Buddhist sutras just means to depart from any phenomenon that man can cognize and to stay in a realm of abstruseness and stillness. It is just the "just-as-it-is-ness" itself, and there are no such distinction of opposite concepts such as "this" and "that", "long" and "short", "high" and "low", "good" and "bad" and so forth, so it is called "non-duality".

Overall, the "gate of non-duality dharma" is an extremely abstruse realm, which Li Hongzhi and his likes should have not been able to understand; he is merely taking it literally and abusing it. Is it not ridiculous?

Buddhism Encourages the Practice of Multiple Gates of Dharma

Now, we can make another question: Does Buddhism ever have any proposition as Li Hongzhi has mentioned: If you have chosen to practice a certain gate of dharma, you should intently focus yourself on that gate of dharma rather than concurrently practicing any other ones.

The answer is absolutely no. Just on the contrary, Buddhism encourages its practitioners to simultaneously practice multiple dharma-gates. Here, the author has three pieces of proof: The first is the "four great vows", the second is the doctrine about "three kinds of wisdom", and the third is the content of scriptures about the practice of Buddhism.

First, the "four great vows". In Buddhism, there are four creeds (targets) that make people to take vows, which are called "Si Hong Shiyuan" (also known as "Si Hong Yuan" 四弘願). It demands a Mahayana novice to solemnly pledge in his mind:

1. I vow to liberate all beings without number.

2. I vow to uproot endless blind passions.
3. I vow to penetrate dharma gates beyond measure.
4. I vow to attain the way of the Buddha.

As it is shown in the third vow that "I vow to penetrate dharma gates beyond measure", not only that Buddhism does not prohibit the practice of other dharma-gates, but also it encourages the practice of all the other dharma-gates. So, evidently Li Hongzhi's talk is completely a fallacy against Buddhism.

Secondly, the doctrine about three kinds of wisdom. Buddhism attaches much importance to wisdom (prajna). In the Mahaprajnaparamita Sastra, there is the wording of "three kinds of wisdom": the wisdom of all things (sarvajna一切智), the wisdom of the seeds of the Way (the wisdom of the bodhisattva道種智), and the knowledge of all knowledge. The wisdom of all Things is the wisdom which a practitioner is able to acquire if only he practices Hinayana (Hearer [Sravaka] and A Buddha on His Own [Pratyekabuddha] 一切種智), the wisdom of the seeds of the Way is what a Mahayana Bodhisattva has to possess, and the knowledge of all knowledge is what only a Buddha can have. In particular, the mainly content of "the wisdom of the seeds of the Way" just means that a Bodhisattva must master all kinds of dharma-gates to practice Buddhism. If it were like Li Hongzhi who limits his disciples to the practice of one single dharma-gate, it would equate to not allowing his disciples to become a Bodhisattva!

Thirdly, the classics about the practice of Buddhism. Buddhism has a lot of classics about its practice, most of which have recorded the methods of cultivation. At present, the most self-contained scripture about Buddhist practice is *The Path of Purification* (清净道論), which has listed 40 kinds of practice methods (Karma-sthana).④ More importantly, no classics have prohibited the practice of more than one dharma-gate; rather, they have encouraged the practice of multiple dharma-gates: a practitioner can choose any gate of dharma that he thinks to suit for him; each person has a different gift, a dharma-gate that suits for others does not necessarily suit himself.

So, it is absolutely wrong as Li Hongzhi restrains all his "disciples" to his only teachings.

Li Hongzhi Has No Confidence in Himself

As a folk adage says, "Nothing is good or bad but by comparison." If one has confidence in his own things, he would be ready to face any comparison rather than fearing it. As it is shown above, however, it is really absurd that Li promiscuously abuses the Buddhist term "non-duality dharma-gate" without knowing its profound meaning and severely prohibits his "disciples" from practicing any other things, and also it indicates that Li has no confidence in his "Dafa".

In practice, Buddhism not only encourages the practice of various Buddhist dharma-gates, but also does not exclude the non-Buddhist practice methods (only if it is not evil). For example, disciples of the Chan School must learn the scriptures of Mahayana Emptiness Sect and Consciousness-only Sect, and meanwhile they can also practice such dharma-gates as the mudras and incantations in Esoteric Buddhism; as a result, the synthetism of the Chan School and the Pure Land has become a tradition of Chinese Buddhism long ago. More than that, the "synthetism of Three Teachings" (Confucianism, Buddhism and Taoism) has been very popular since the Ming Dynasty, and thus produced many new sects, which have not been excluded by the traditional Buddhism. As early as in the times of Sakyamuni, Buddhism had been well known for its treating all the other thoughts both kindly and equally, the so-called "Six Kinds of Heresy" （六師外道）at that time have also been included into many copies of Buddhist sutras. so, Buddhism is a religion that has shown more tolerance and freedom than any others; many scholars in the early modern times (Liang Qichao 梁啓超, Zhang Taiyan 章太炎, Xiong Shili熊十力, Mou Zongsan牟宗三, Fang Dongmei 方東美, Tang Junyi 唐君毅and so on) even viewed the thoughts of Buddhism as philosophy (the learning of Buddhism), and that is also acceptable. As the saying goes that "acceptance makes greatness" （有容乃大）, Buddhism has shown more tolerance and freedom than any other religions; hence it is able to develop into a world religion.

Overall, Li Hongzhi is so superficial, but he asserts, "Falun Dafa is not a religion, but people in the future will think it a religion," and "You must understand that the practice pattern that I leave with you is unchangeable, you shall not do what I do not, you shall not use what I do not, and you shall talk in the way I talk in the practice. Take care! To change Fofa without noticing it is to destroy it the same way." ⑤ That evidently indicates what a small-minded man he is and how he brags unblushingly.

Notes:

1. *Falun Dafa Interpretation*, pp. 56—57.
2. *Zhuan Falun*, pp. 113-114.
3. 3. The above quotations come from the Chapter of Entrance into Non-duality Dharma-gate（入不二法門品）in the *Vimalakirti Sutra*, annotated by Kumarajiva and his disciple Monk Zhao.
4. As for the content of *The Path of Purification*, see the 6th chapter of the author's *Selection of Buddhist Doctrines*. Shanghai Ancient Book Press, 2009, 1st print run, distributed by the Taipei Lao Ku Culture Foundation Inc.
5. *Essentials for Further Advances*, pp. 92 & 106.

From "Latter Dharma" to "True Dharma"

In many of his lectures and writings in the early period (before April 1999), Li Hongzhi had called this period a "period of latter dharma" （末法時期）. On April 25, 1999, Li mobilized ten thousand Falun Gong disciples to besiege Zhongnanhai in Beijing, demonstrating in silence to the CPC Central Committee; afterwards, the writings that he published (most are included into the *Falun Fofa—Essentials for Further Advances* [Vol. Two]) modify his previous remarks, wantonly calling this period "the period of true dharma" （正法時期）. Such modification is not noticed by common people; but those of insight know that there must be some mystery in it. In general, it has two purposes:

1. To highlight his arrogant mentality to surpass Chinese Buddhism and even the Buddha; and
2. To encourage his disciples to bravely put up political struggles against the CPC.

The modification of one single noun has involved so profound intention; the common people can hardly see it through because they do not know the difference between "the period of true dharma" and the period of "latter dharma". Li is capable indeed because he has a meticulous mind; and his serious shortcoming rests in his arrogance and his ignorance. That is a huge disparity between desires and wisdom, which the ancient Chinese people had described as "*zhi da cai shu*" (志大才疏 to hitch one's wagon to a star).

The Theory about Three Periods in Buddhism

Some Buddhist scriptures contain the expression "three periods": once a Buddha emerges in the world, the evolution of Buddhism will experience three stages, namely "the period of true dharma", "the period of semblance dharma" and "the period of latter dharma". A Buddha's edification can be divided into three parts: teachings (the instruction in words or scriptures, mainly the theoretical part), practices (the actions to put theories into practice, suggesting the part of practices and cultivation) and demonstration (the demonstration of achievements, i.e., the obtainment of the achieved statuses of Arhat, Bodhisattva or even Buddha when a practitioner reaches a certain realm). In the period of true dharma, the three of teachings, practices and demonstration are all available, and this period is also the stage with the most powerful edification. In the period of semblance dharma, as its name shows, it seems that there were "dharma": both teachings and practices are available, but there is no demonstration anymore. While it comes to "the period of latter dharma", there are left a muddle of theories made by the Buddha, neither practices or demonstration is available.①

As for the lengths of the three periods of "true dharma", "semblance dharma" and "latter dharma", scriptures disagree with each other. In general, the period of "true dharma" refers to the days when Sakyamuni lived in this world and the five hundred years after his nirvana; the period of "semblance dharma" refers to the age of a thousand years after that, and the period of "latter dharma" refers to that of ten thousand years after the period of "semblance dharma". Because the Buddha lived 2,500 years ago, Buddhism frequently mentions the present as the period of "latter dharma".

The Purpose to Stress "Latter Dharma"

Li Hongzhi stresses that it is now "the period of latter dharma", which refers to the period of latter dharma of Buddhism, and also a period of degenerate morality. Actually, he intends to stress the degradation of times to highlight the superiority of "Falun Fofa" and its compliance with the need of the times. He says,

> "Our Falun Dafa is one of the eighty-four thousand dharma-gates, and has no relation to primitive Buddhism or the Buddhism in the period of Latter Dharma, nor is it related to the religions at present."

> "Latter Dharma not only means that Buddhism is in the period of latter dharma, but also that the human society has no spiritual law to maintain its morality anymore."

> "At present, I am the only one to propagate true dharma all over the world, I have done a thing that the predecessors have never done, and more importantly, I have established such an important dharma-gate in the period of latter dharma. It is really once in a blue moon…"

> "This is the last time when we propagate true dharma in the period of latter dharma."②

He even derogates Sakyamuni's Buddhism as "at the very low level", and the monastics even cannot rescue themselves:

> "Sakyamuni's Buddhism was propagated for the mediocre people at very low levels 2,500 years ago, that is, the people who had come from the primitive society and had simple minds. And the period of latter dharma in his term just refers to the present, for Sakyamuni's dharma does not suit for today's people anymore. In the period of latter dharma, Buddhist monastics even cannot rescue themselves, let alone others."③

All Gods Are Inferior to Li Hongzhi

Therefore, Li Hongzhi thinks himself the only "Buddha of today" (Living Buddha), and far superior to Sakyamuni and the "masters" of all sects in the history; this is a great period, a "period of true dharma" centered on Li Hongzhi. Hence, from June 2000, he simply calls his "Fa" (dharma) the "Hongchuan Dafa" (洪传大法 Dafa Propagated by Li Hongzhi);④ in other words, he uses his own name as the name of his "dharma". At the same time, he has been publicly propagating that it is now "the period of true dharma".

First, let's have a look at how he fabricates the history of world religion:

> "Then, we have a look at it from the point of history. The 卐 design has also been found in the ancient Greek culture excavated by the Western society. As a matter of fact, people in the very ancient times before the Flood also believed in the Buddha…In fact, what Brahmanism believed in at first was also the Buddha, and it was the inheritance of the Buddha that the antediluvian Greeks believed in, at that time they called the Buddha as the God…More than a thousand years later in the ancient India, Brahmanism entered its period of latter dharma, and people began to embrace miscellaneous beliefs except the Buddha…By the time when Sakyamuni emerged in the world, Brahmanism had completely degraded into an evil cult."

The above so-called "history" is completely nonsense! Any history must be based on evidence (including literature, archeological proof, and even the legends coming down from previous generations). When Sakyamuni established Buddhism, he himself was esteemed as "Buddha" (the Enlightened), this is a part of authentic history proven by numberless evidence, how can Li fabricate that the ancient Greeks and Brahmanism also believed in the Buddha?

Then, he continues to blather,

> "I wonder if you know that a Taoist immortal is one kind of God, the Buddha is one kind of God, and Jehovah, Jesus and St. Mary are kinds of Gods, only that they are at different levels and have different forms due to their different cultivation goals

and their different cognition of the cosmic law. The enormous celestial bodies were created by Fofa, not by those such as the Buddha, Taoist immortals or Gods..."

This is declaring that Taoist immortals, the Buddha, Jehovah, Jesus and St. Mary are gods or goddess who have made certain achievements by "practicing Dafa"! Those gods were unable to create the universe, of course, and Jehovah, the God of Christianity, did not, either. Why was that? He explains it clearly in a short essay titled "Profundity" (博大) in the *Essentials for Further Advances*:

"Falun Dafa...is the true dharma that has never been propagated...It surpasses all the learning and ethics in the mediocre society from the very ancient time to the present. What the previous religions propagandized and people perceived in the past were merely semblance and superficial knowledge."

Even Jehovah the God was merely "semblance". All the Gods were inferior to Li Hongzhi, and the enormous universe and the enormous celestial bodies in it were created by Li's "Fofa".

And then, he derogates the modern Buddhism in this "period of latter dharma" as has been very similar with the Brahmanism that turned out to be a cult in those days!

"As a matter of fact, Sakyamuni had described the state of the period of latter dharma already, and what is the difference between the modern Buddhism and the later Brahmanism?"

At last, Li Hongzhi expresses what he really wants to! Now it is the time when Li, the greatest God or Buddha, emerges in this world "once again" to propagate the greatest "fundamental cosmic law". In other words, it is the high time of Li's "period of true dharma"!

"Now, I have come to this world once again for the propaganda of dharma, and more importantly, I am now directly propagating the fundamental cosmic law...The universe follows the rule

*of formation, existence and extinction, nothing can keep unchanged, and there are Buddhas emerging in this world to rescue human beings in each period. That is how the history develops, and the mankind in future will be able to hear about Fofa the same way."*⑤

Li is so audacious as to fabricate in such a way the history of how "Fofa" emerged in the world. Obviously he does not know what "history" is, possibly he thinks any of his nonsense can be viewed as history, so he brags shamelessly "that is how the history develops". Here, the author advises Master Li snatches a little time to consult the related chapters and passages in the *Shi Ji* (史记the *Records of the Grand Historian*) by Sima Qian(司馬遷), a historian of the Han Dynasty, and such authoritative works as the *Shi Tong* (史通 the *Generality of Historiography*) by Liu Zhiji(劉知幾), a historian of the Tang Dynasty, the Wenshi Tongyi (文史通義*On Literature and History* by Zhang Xuecheng(章學誠), a scholar of the Qing Dynasty, and the Zhongguo Lishi Yanjiu Fangfa (中國歷史研究法The *Methods of Chinese History Studies*) by Liang Qichao(梁啓超), a modern scholar. Having done so, perhaps he, who is fond of apprenticing others, would not fabricate history like this anymore in case he lays himself open to ridicule by teaching his "disciples" wrongly.

The Instigation of Political Opposition

After the "April 25th Incident", "Falun Gong" has been banned in the mainland of China, hence the writings that Li published after that frequently stress "true dharma" or "the period of true dharma", prompt the disciples overseas to take advantage of all chances to oppose the CPC, and encourage those in the mainland to stand up with "the most severe test". These writings have included into the *Falun Fofa—Essentials for Further Advances* (Vol. Two). Now let's quote a few paragraphs as evidence:

"In the period of true dharma, trainees have done very well; especially, the trainees in Russia have established Buddhist

societies under various pressures and played a great role in telling the truth although the Russian people have been seriously swayed by the propaganda of the evil political group of China. These are all great. I hope this Buddhist assembly will be helpful in telling the truth, disclosing evils and rescuing all the living beings. You should frequently communicate with trainees in other regions abroad, encouraging each other and progressing together."⑥

By saying this, he tries to ferment his international disciples to put up political opposition.

"If you have not made it clear what a disciple of true dharma is even by now, you will not be able to get out of the current disasters...The greatness of Dafa disciples just rests in that you live together with your master in this period of true dharma and are thus able to protect Dafa."

"Now, the disciples of Dafa are in the period of true dharma, and the old forces have formed the most fundamental and most severe test to the disciples of Dafa, whether you can get through such a test...has become a standard for the consummate qualification of a disciple of true dharma, and the difference between mortal and immortal."⑦

This is the guideline of political activities for instigating the disciples in mainland of China in this "period of true dharma".

"If a practitioner can give no thought to life or death at any circumstance, evils must be afraid of him; if all the trainees can manage to do so, the evil will perish by itself."⑧

"Forbearance is absolutely not unlimited connivance which allows such evils as have completely lost their humanity and right mind...If the evil has developed to an irremediable extent, it will be necessary to adopt different forms at different levels *to stop or eradicate it...The eradication of the evil is for the sake of the true dharma, and it is not a matter of personal practice."*⑨

With this, he takes a further step to call on his disciples to "give no thought to life or death" and "eradicate the evil".

Li Hongzhi's "Glorious Birthday"

Li Hongzhi was born on May 13, 1951. That day happened to be the 8th day of the 4th month in the traditional Chinese calendar, and Chinese Buddhism traditionally views this date as the birthday of the Buddha. On July 23, 1999, the *People's Daily* in the mainland published an essay authored by Zhang Husheng, pointing out that Li's real birthday was July 7, 1952, and that not until September 24, 1994 did he alter his birthday to be the Buddha's birthday the previous year. The essay comes to a conclusion that Li even faked his birthday to fabricate the miracle of "the reincarnation of the Buddha" and so on. Almost at the same time, Li published an essay titled A Brief Statement of Mine in the USA to clarify this matter:

*"Some people started a rumor that I have altered my birthday, it is a fact. But another fact is that the government registered my birthday wrongly in the Cultural Revolution, and I simply altered the wrong date of my birthday back to the correct one. As for the remark that Sakyamuni was also born at that date, but what relation does it have with me? There have been many criminals who were born that day! And moreover, I have never said I am Sakyamuni."*⑩

Did Li Hongzhi alter his birthday? It is a matter of triviality, and Li's refutation seems to be reasonable, too. But the point is that Li's many writings have proven that he has professed the "Fofa" which he has propagated is more consummate than and superior to what Sakyamuni did. The Buddhism that Sakyamuni established in those days has become a "cult" like Brahmanism in "the period of latter dharma", so Li is needed to come to this world "again" to propagate "true dharma".

Confucius said that it was necessary to observe a person's practical actions in addition to his remarks when we judge him. (Gongye Chang 公冶長 in the *Analects of Confucius*, "I used to take a man at his words and trusted he would act accordingly. But now I listen to his words and note his actions.") Now, let's have a look at Li's latest action.

According to the 174th issue of the *New Epoch Weekly* (新纪元 周刊published on May 27, 2010), May 13 this year was Li Hongzhi's 59th "glorious birthday". The journal says,

> *"Falun Gong trainees and the multitude all over the world expressed their congratulations in succession to Master Li Hongzhi, the initiator of Falun Gong, and the sight of the world was focused on Master Li once again."*

It is so ludicrous and disgusting to unrestrainedly "celebrate glorious birthday" when one is merely 59 years old! In the Chinese tradition of filial piety, a virtuous man did celebrate his birthday for himself, for his birthday just meant his mother's "hardest day", and any celebration would mean a breach of filial piety. When he was very aged (above 70 years old), his own parents were not alive anymore, and he himself had both children and grandchildren; these children would perform birthday activities for him to show their filial pieties, but still some virtuous people would "evade birthday celebrations". How can one in his fifties publicly celebrate his birthday in such a big way? If one passes away in his fifties, it would be an early death in modern times, and cannot be viewed as "longevity" at all, so it appears more ridiculous to call it "glorious birthday".

In the recent 60 years, Mr. Chiang Kai-shek was the only personage who publicly celebrated his birthday, and other great personages such as Mao Zedong, Deng Xiaoping and Chiang Ching-kuo all prohibited others to hold birthday celebrations for them. Mr. Nan Huaijin, a world-known leading authority of the Chan School, is 95 years old already, but he has never accepted any celebrations from his disciples, and he even does not allow his family to prepare any birthday banquet for him. Mr. Chiang, who was 75 years old soon after he came to Taiwan, exceptionally allowed all circles to perform the activities of "congratulations to Master Kiang's Great Birthday" on October 31 every year until his death when he was 88 years old. But he did so not completely for the sake of "personal worship". In fact, Taiwan was in a precarious situation at that time; in order to withstand Mao Zedong, it was necessary to "cement the center of leadership" by means of such birthday celebration. But what a man is Li Hongzhi? He is only in his fifties, but unexpectedly he "celebrated his glorious birthday" in such a big way! Such ridiculous activity is enough to indicate what a man he is.

If he sees the author's refutation and analysis above, he will argue, of course, "It was my disciples who did it, and it has nothing to do with me." But he must not forget that he has given public notice for several times that any report on him shall not be published without his approval (see details above in the 7th section titled "Foolish Mirages"). Especially, the *New Epoch Weekly* is nothing but a journal of his own "Falun Gong" organization, so it is equivalent to that he celebrated his "glorious birthday" by himself.

The *Diamond Sutra*（金剛經） says, "Once a Bodhisattva clings to the idea of self, others, living being or longevity, he is no longer a bodhisattva."（若菩薩有我相、人相、眾生相、壽者相，即非菩薩）Li celebrated his birthday although he is merely in his fifties; this is unusual obduracy to the "idea of longevity". Moreover, he is more obdurate to the "idea of self" (thinking he himself really stands for the highest principle of the universe), the "idea of others" (thinking that all the other people are inferior to him, and that he has even surpassed the God Jehovah, Jesus, the Buddha, Confucius, Laotze and so on), and the "idea of living beings" (thinking that all the living beings can make proper achievements only by being his disciples). What kind of "true dharma" could a man of such obduracy propagate?

Notes:

1. This theory comes from the *Analysis and Appreciation of the Lotus Sutra*, which says, "As for the true dharma of the Buddha, teachings, practice and demonstration are all contained; as for the semblance dharma of the Buddha, there are only teachings and practice without demonstration, and as for the latter dharma of the Buddha, both practice and demonstration are in lack." Quoted from the *Grand Buddhist Dictionary*, the entry of "zheng xiang mo" （正像末條.）

2. *Zhuan Falun*, pp. 107, 112, 115 & 150.

3. Ibid, p. 14.

4. *Falun Fofa—Essentials for Further Advances* (Vol. Two), p. 31.

5. *Falun Fofa—Essentials for Further Advances*, pp. 146-149.

6. *Falun Fofa—Essentials for Further Advances* (Vol. Two), p. 115, the essay titled A Speech to the Second Session of Dafa Assembly in Russia.

7. Ibid, pp. 103-109, the essay titled the Disciples of Dafa in the True Dharma Period.

8. Ibid, p. 43.

9. Ibid, pp. 48-49.

10. Ibid, p. 15.

The Castigation against the Chan School

The Chan School （禪宗）is a Buddhist sect with the most outstanding Chinese characteristics, and has been viewed as a representative of Chinese Buddhism over a thousand years. The Chan School has extended its influence all over many East Asian countries including Japan, Korea and Viet Nam as early as in the Song Dynasty （宋朝）, and deeply into the circles of thoughts and arts in European and American countries in the early modern times. So, the Chan School is a pride of the Chinese culture and of the Chinese people. However, Li Hongzhi takes advantage of every chance to denounce the Chan School, as if he would feel unhappy if he did not do so. Why is it on earth?

He Can Propagate His "Hongfa" (洪法) Only by Inveighing against the Chan School

Li Hongzhi says,

"Still I want to stress a question: We are going to teach Gong and propagate dharma when we practice. Some Buddhist monastics, especially the monastics of the Chan School, may have some reluctance; they would be reluctant to listen to us once we begin to propagate dharma. Why is that? Because the Chan School thinks that this dharma cannot be articulated; in their opinion, the dharma cannot be dharma anymore once it

*is articulated, so there is no dharma that can be propagated, and one can understand it only tacitly. Hence, the Chan School cannot propagate any dharma until today."*①

Li Hongzhi constantly stresses his "dharma" is the only key point; his so-called "dharma", however, is nothing but his feigned theory. Buddhist monastics know some Buddhist learning more or less, so they would know Li is talking nonsense at the hearing of his "dharma". Li thinks this is the most serious hindrance of his "Hongfa". Meanwhile, the Buddhist monastics in China mostly belong to the Chan School, for example, the famous Master Hsing Yun(星雲)at the Fo Guang Shan（佛光山） in Taiwan is just a successor of the 48th generation of the Linji Sect(臨濟宗) of the Chan School; therefore, Li certainly attacks the Chan School to spread his own "Fofa". More than that, the Chan School has represented the Chinese Buddhism over a thousand years, so, the castigation against the Chan School has naturally become a means to elevate himself.

Li Hongzhi denounces the Pure Land Sect（净土宗）, too:

*"Now, what do the monastics of the Chan School read at present? They even read the Amitabha Sutra（阿彌陀經）, so they have no ethos of the Chan School anymore. The dharma of the Chan School does not exist in the world anymore."*②

According to historical literature, Buddhism was introduced into China in the late Western Han Dynasty the first century B. C., and it took more than 700 years to finally meet its prosperity in the Sui and Tang dynasties. This period can be divided into three stages: the first stage featured "the introduction of beliefs", which lasted about 300 years; the second stage was mainly focused on the "introduction of doctrines", which lasted more than 200 years; and the third stage was centered on "development and creation", which lasted more than 200 years. Chinese Buddhism met its summit in the times of Emperor Xuanzong（玄宗712-756) of the middle Tang Dynasty; afterwards, due to frequent turbulences and wars, as well as the "Huichang Suppression of Buddhism"（會昌法難） during the reign of Emperor Wuzong (武宗840--846) of the Tang Dynasty, all the other Buddhist sects declined except the Chan School and the Pure Land prevalent among folks. The Pure Land is a kind of practice mainly centered on the chanting of "Amitabha Buddha", which is simple and can be easily practiced, so it has been widely accepted among folks. After the Song Dynasty, the Chan School and the Pure Land were integrated, so the monastics of the Chan School in China began to concurrently practice the chanting of the title of Amitabha Buddha of the Pure Land. Overall, from the late Tang Dynasty to the present, the so-called "Chinese Buddhism" is mainly the Chan School and the Pure Land Sect. Therefore, Li has actually denounced all the Buddhist believers in China when he defiantly denounces the Chan School and the *Amitabha Sutra* as the principal scripture of the Pure Land sect.

Mistakes about the History of the Chan School

Li Hongzhi, who is fond of castigating the Chan School, has made mistakes about the history of the Chan School although it is very simple. Now, let's have a look at two passages from his writings:

*"Bodhidharma himself said that his dharma would continue only up to the Sixth Hierarch, and it would not do after the latter. Now, hundreds of years have passed, but some people still clang to the doctrines of the Chan School."*③

*"The dharma-gate of the Chan School does not exist anymore; more than that, it is not that it begins to dissolve today, rather, it had dissolved into nothing as early as when it came to Huineng the Six Hierarch. It had extinguished hundreds of years ago, and what is left today is merely the history."*④

In these two passages, Li has made three mistakes:
1. How would Bodhidharma say his teachings "would continue only up to the Sixth Hierarch"? This is merely Li's groundless nonsense.

There is very little literature about Bodhidharma, and most of the extant one is the fabrication of later generations. A legend has it that Bodhidharma left a verse at the end of his life, which says,

I came to this land, (吾本來茲土)
To propagate dharma and rescue the confused sentient beings.
(傳法救迷情)
With one flower producing five leaves, (一花開五葉)
It fruits in a natural course. (结果自然成)

Some people hold that the line "with one flower producing five leaves" in the verse suggests that the Chan School developed into the five sects of Fayan (法眼), Yunmen (雲門), Cao-Dong (曹洞), Linji (臨濟) and Wei-Yang (潙仰) after Huineng the Sixth Hierarch, some others argue that it means the lineage through five generations from Bodhidharma himself to Huineng. At any rate, however, these two explanations are untenable: Bodhidharma was not an immortal in folk supernatural stories, how could he foresee the things five generations later? Even if he could, still Li is wrong when he alleges that "Bodhidharma himself said that his dharma would continue only up to the Sixth Hierarch, and it would not do after the latter", for no one but the Sixth Hierarch was the true initiator of the Chan School, how can one say "it would not do" after him? The very reason that the Chan School dates its origin back to Bodhidharma and even to the 28 ancestral hierarchs is merely that later generations wanted to justify their theory by fabricating a glorious lineage.

2. It was not "hundreds of years". The Sixth Hierarch Huineng (六祖慧能) was born in 638 and died in 713, from the reign of Emperor Taizong (唐太宗626--649) to that of Xuanzong, and it is as long as 1,300 years up to now. Li says that "hundreds of years have passed", obviously he has shortened this period too much.
3. The dharma-gate of the Chan School is not the case that "it had dissolved into nothing as early as when it came to Huineng the Six Hierarch". Exactly on the contrary, the Chan School did

not really begin until the days of Huineng, for Huineng was the very one who established the Chan School of China. Actually, the Chan School was divided as the southern sect and the northern one, the northern sect had Shenxiu(神秀) as its representative, and the southern sect was established by Huineng. The northern sect laid an emphasis on gradual cultivation, and the south sect promoted sudden enlightenment. The northern Chan prospered in the days of Wu Zetian (690--705), and vanished within a hundred years. The southern Chan（南禪）, however, has not only developed into five sects, but come down through 1,300 years up to now, and extended its influence to Japan, Korea, Viet Nam and many other countries in the modern world. In a word, from the late Tang Dynasty, the so-called "Chinese Buddhism" has mainly had the Chan School as its representative, and the so-called "Chan School" has been actually the southern Chan initiated by Huineng. However, Li Hongzhi alleges that "it had dissolved into nothing as early as when it came to the Six Hierarch Huineng"; evidently he knows nothing about the history of the Chan School.⑤

He Feigned the Origin of the Chan School

What was the origin of the Chan School? A traditional story goes like this: once upon a time, the Buddha propagated his dharma at the Eagle Mountain, but he merely picked up a piece of flower, saying nothing to the disciples in his presence. No disciples but Kashyap understood the Buddha's meaning, and the latter was the only one who smiled at sight of the Buddha's action. Immediately the Buddha knew that Kashyap was able to take over his cause, so he declared on site to his disciples, *"I have a collection of views of right dharma, which is characterized with the wonderful mind of nirvana. It reveals the reality whose essence is non-reality, and it is a delicate gate leading to the dharma. It does not depend upon any language or words, and it will be passed on in a form different from the existing one of Buddhism. Now, I have passed it on to Mahakashyap."⑥*

Li does not seem to know the above mentioned literature at all, and he feigned as follows instead,

"Bodhidharma's propaganda of the Chan School was based on Sakyamuni's one single remark. Sakyamuni said, 'Fa wu ding fa（法無定法）.' He just established the dharma-gate of the Chan School on the basis of this remark of Sakyamuni."

The author wonders in what book Li found his evidence, if he cannot give any proof, he would be fabricating a myth. Actually, some Buddhist books do contain the sentence that *"fa wu ding fa"*, but it means "the practice shall not be limited to a certain dharma-gate"; that is what Li hates most, so he strictly demands his "disciples" from time to time to practice only the "Dafa" that he has prescribed rather than mixing it with any other dharma-gates (See the 13th section "What Is Non-duality Dharma-gate" above). Perhaps just because of this reason, he inexplicably transplanted the sentence that *"fa wu ding fa"* to the origin of the Chan School.

Li Does Not Understand the Doctrines of the Chan School

Li continues,

"We hold that this dharma-gate is just getting itself into a dead end. Why do we call it getting into a dead end? When Bodhidharma got into it, it seemed quite capacious anyhow; when the Second Hierarch got in, it became less broad; when the Third Hierarch got in, it still felt okay anyhow; when the Fourth Hierarch got in, it had become rather narrow; when it came to the Fifth Hierarch, there had almost been no room left for him; and at the times of the Sixth Hierarch Huineng, it had come to its very limitation, and he was not able to get in anymore...Now, hundreds of years have passed, but some people still clung to the doctrines of the Chan School...
"At last, Sakyamuni said, 'I have not propagated any dharma all my life.' Again, the Chan School misunderstands it as there is no dharma that can be propagated...In the past, many people, especially those of the Chan School, had embraced such prejudice and extremely wrong cognition. Not being taught,

*how can you direct others to practice? How to practice? How to cultivate yourself?"*⑦

The two passages quoted above obviously indicate that Li Hongzhi does not understand the doctrines of the Chan School. Why does the author say so? Now let's summarize the doctrines of the Chan School as the following few points to explain it briefly:

1. The major idea of the Chan School is to directly start with our "mind", the origin of all dharma to seek for emancipation, and that is what is meant by such expression as to "directly point to the mind and achieve Buddhahood by seeing through the nature" (直指人心，見性成佛). Therefore, the Chan School is also called "Xin Zong"(心宗the Sect of Mind). Here, the so-called "all dharma" refer to all things (both material and non-material) in the universe that our minds cognize, perceive, imagine and even anticipate. All such things cannot be separated from the minds of human beings.⑧ Especially, the affliction and pleasure are more obviously the feelings of our minds, and completely depend upon the minds of human beings. The Chan School just teaches people to directly make efforts on our "minds"; so long as we can understand and grasp the "nature" in our minds that is not restrained by anything, we will achieve the goal of our cultivation (the achievement of Buddhahood). Such practice is known as to "enlighten the mind and see the nature".

2. The so-called "nature" (性) refers to a kind of vacant realm of our minds, i.e., the frame of mind that "involves no good or evil, and no purity or impurity", the realm of transcendence over anything. As the *Diamond Sutra* says, one should have his mind clinging to nothing; that just means such a realm. This kind of realm is the top quality of our mind, and it is the realm of "the ultimate emptiness" (畢竟空).

3. The problem is that it is not difficult to "see through the nature" occasionally or for a short time, but it is uneasy to hold this "nature" in the mind and keep the same way for long (clinging to nothing); for our minds keep changing all the time in response to various situations outside, and that is what the so-called "thought-moment" （念頭） means; they do not stop even when we are sleeping (dreaming is also thought). According to the *Renwang Jing (*仁王經*Humane King Sutra)*, one single thought of a mind consists of 90 moments, and in each moment there are 900 times emergence and extinction, that is, there are 81,000 times emergence and extinction in one single thought moment. That indicates how difficult to ascertain the "changes of ideas", and how difficult it is to grasp the realm of "nature"! Therefore, the Chan School expends its efforts right at this point.

4. Just because the efforts are made on such "minds", the teaching methods may vary due to the different characters, dispositions, knowledge and insights of each individual; that is what is meant by "administering doses as occasion requires" and "*fa wu ding fa*"（法無定法）. In other words, the teaching methods of the Chan School are very flexible; it may make use of any methods, and is not restrained by anything. It may use any methods that may help "enlighten the mind and see the nature"（明心見性）, for example, to make gestures, to be enlightened by discourse, to grasp the thread of discourse and even to hit with staff and teach; and it may get rid of anything that may be unhelpful to "the enlightenment of the mind and the cognition of the nature", including the recitation of sutras, the worship of the Buddha and legs-crossed sitting in meditation. The Chan School even allows the scolding of the Buddha and the ancestral hierarchs.

5. The Chan School is proud of itself because it does "not depend upon any words"（不立文字）, but in fact, it has

enormous writings about itself. For example, the most outstanding representative is the one-hundred-volume *Zongjinglu* (宗鏡錄Records of Principle and Mirror) written and compiled by Yanshou of the North Song Dynasty (北宋延寿禪師), which flaunts to "hold one mind as a principle, and reflect all dharma as a mirror". It cites more than 300 sutras and explanatory treatises, and quotes the quintessence of all the other schools and sects to demonstrate the issue of "mind". So, it is not that the Chan School pays no attention to scriptures or explanatory treatises, let alone that "there is no dharma to propagate"; it is only that it does not restrain itself with any classical dharma-gate. That is what is meant by the sentence that "the Way must penetrate and flow, and the mind does not dwell in dharma. The mind that dwells in dharma is in self-bondage". Li knows nothing about the above-mentioned, so he surprisingly utters such expressions as "getting into the dead end". That indicates he does not know the Chan School at all.

6. Just as Tang Junyi said, the Sixth Hierarch Huineng had made a creative "new synthetism" of the doctrines of Buddhism—he integrated the existing "spirit of pranja" (the thought of the Emptiness Sect with Nagarjuna as a representative) in India, the doctrines of sects (Tiantai and Huayan sects) established in China at that time, and the quintessence theory of "man's original mind" stressed both by traditional Chinese Confucianism and Taoism. It is absolutely not accidental that the Chan School established by Huineng turned out to be the mainstay of Chinese Buddhism afterwards.⑨ However, Li Hongzhi alleges that "it had dissolved into nothing as early as when it came to Huineng the Six Hierarch"; obviously he does not know what the Chan School is.

Overall, Li fabricates the history of the Chan School and denounces it from time to time while he actually knows nothing about it. Why does he do so? The very reasons just rest in the following two points:

1. The Chan School is the representative of Chinese Buddhism, and to castigate the Chan School just means to improve his own status; and

2. The Chan School is the most typical "self-reliance religion", but Li Hongzhi attempts to establish an "others-reliance religion" which reveres himself as "the only true God"; the existence of the Chan School predestines Li's frustration.⑩

Notes:
1. *Zhuan Falun*, p. 11.
2. *Falun Dafa Interpretation*, p. 101.
3. *Zhuan Falun*, p. 11.
4. *Falun Dafa Interpretation*, p. 101.
5. *The History of the Chan School* written by Rev. Yinshun印順 is an authoritative work in modern times. Those who want to deeply research the Chan School can consult this book. It has been published both in Taiwan and the mainland, and readers can find information on it in the internet.
6. See the *Compilation of Five Lam s*（五燈會元）, Vol. 1. It is also recorded in the *Record of the Transmission of the Lamp Published in the Jingde Era*（景德傳燈錄）, Vol. 1.
7. *Zhuan Falun*, pp. 11-13.
8. A common sense holds that no objective things such as mountains, rivers and lands are related to the mind of man; but Buddhism argues that it is a wrong opinion. It is not easy to completely understand this issue, and it would be helpful to have the basic knowledge of Kant's philosophy.

9. See Tang Junyi, the Research on the Origin of Nature in the *Research on the Origin of Chinese Philosophy*（唐君毅：中國哲學原論・原性篇）, Chapter 10, p. 299 and infra. Taiwan Student Book Co., Ltd., 1991, the revised edition of complete collection.

10. All the religions in the world can be divided into the two types of "others-reliance" and "self-reliance". The former asks to believe in a target except oneself (for example, God, deities and the Buddha) to protect himself, whereas the latter is exactly on the contrary. According to the latter type of religion, a believer does not need to rely on any external sacred targets, and one can reach the realm of gods or the Buddha so long he gives a play to his own "original nature" and relies on his own power to practice. The most typical others-reliance religion is Christianity in the West (including Catholic, Protestant and Oriental Orthodox churches), and the Chan School of Buddhism is a pure kind of self-reliance religion. Falun Gong that Li established stubbornly asks believers to believe in his "Dafa", it is actually a kind of other-reliance religion resembling Christianity. A self-reliance religion tallies with the traditional Chinese culture, and thus can easily develop in China; others-reliance religions are on the contrary, for example, Christianity had been introduced into China as early as in the Tang Dynasty, but did not develop until the middle Qing Dynasty; only up to the late Qing Dynasty, it took advantage of the military superiority of the Western powers to enter China once again, resulting in the small scale at present.

What Is "the Dual Cultivation of Xing and Ming"?

Li Hongzhi often boasts that his "Dafa" belongs to the type of "the dual cultivation of *xing*性 and *ming*命", much superior to Buddhism which cultivates mere "*xing*" (nature or quality) and Taoism which cultivates mere "*ming*" (destiny or life). As a matter of fact, his so-called "dual cultivation" is a plagiary from *A Genuine Taoist Guide to Cultivation of Nature and Life*（仙踪性命圭旨）, a Taoist classic. Especially in the traditional Chinese culture, the two terms "*xing*" and "*ming*" have very profound meanings, which are probably beyond Li's understanding, and he is just deceiving people with them.

Now, let's have a look at how Li preaches.

"The dual cultivation of xing and ming just means that a practitioner cultivates ming while he cultivates his mind and nature, that is, to improve a practitioner's physical health and transform his nature. In the process of such transformation, the cells of the practitioner's body will slow down the aging courses when they are gradually replaced with high energy substances. The physical body will return to the condition of younger ages; it returns slowly, and transforms gradually, until it was completely replaced with high energy substances at last. At that time, the physical body of that man has completely

turned into the form composed of other kinds of substances. In this case, the new body will have gotten out of the restraints of the Five Elements as I have mentioned; not restrained by the Five Elements, his body will be an everlasting one.

"Buddhist monastics cultivate mere nature when they practice, so they pay no attention to mudras or the cultivation of ming; they stress nirvana...

*"Taoists lay an emphasis on the cultivation of ming, for they choose disciples and do not talk the rescue of all living beings. What they face are very kind people, so they talk about such things as magic arts, they pay attention to the issue of how to cultivate ming."*①

In Volume Yuan of *A Genuine Taoist Guide to Cultivation of Nature and Life*, there are special passages about the "theory about *xing* and *ming*" and an "illustration of consummation of *xing* and *ming*", both of which explain in detail the issue of "dual cultivation of *xing* and *ming*"; obviously, the above passages quoted from Li's writings are plagiary from this book, merely added with some modern scientific terms such as "high energy substances".

A Genuine Taoist Guide to Cultivation of Nature and Life, however, is the synthetism of Confucianism, Buddhism and Taoism, hence is fairly profound and deserves to take as a reference. For example, it says,

"Xing differs as the quality of physical forms and the nature endowed by the Heaven, and ming varies as the ming of destiny and the ming of physical forms. A gentleman cultivates the nature endowed by the Heaven and overcomes the quality of physical forms, and cultivates the ming of physical forms and commits himself to the ming as destiny."

Here, the so-called "the quality of physical forms, the nature endowed by the Heaven, the *ming* of destiny and the *ming* of physical forms" actually sourced from the thoughts of Confucianism. The "nature endowed by the Heaven" is just the nature in the sentence that "the Heavenly mandate is called nature", the beginning sentence in the *Doctrine of the Mean* (中庸), and also the nature in Mencius' idea that "man is good in nature" (人性善);② this kind of "nature" is totally good. The "quality of physical forms" is the nature of a man that determines him as an animal, and the nature in the sentence that "appetite and sexuality belong to the category of nature" in Gaozi告子's term; this kind of nature contains both good and non-good. The so-called "*ming* of physical forms" suggests the life of a man's physical body; the life of a man mainly rests in his physical body, so the cultivation of "*ming* of physical forms" just means the exercise of a physical body. In comparison, the "*ming* of destiny" is much more complicated. It is the "destiny" as Confucius said in the sentence that he "cannot be a superior man without knowing destiny" (不知命無以為君子), and also the "*ming*" we frequently talk in the sentence that one "endeavors to the utmost and accepts the arrangement of the Heaven" (盡人事而聽天命); this kind of "*ming*" is beyond man's capability and yet has to be faced, hence Mou Zongsan (牟宗三) described it as "not an empirical concept, nor a concept in man's knowledge; instead, it is a virtual concept in practice…It seems to be a ghost; you cannot grasp it, but it is a negative kind of entity indeed, and you have to face it."③ As for this kind of "*ming*" that is beyond man's capability, Mencius also remarked that a man had no way but "cultivate himself to anticipate it" (修身以俟之). Therefore, the word "commit" in the expression to "commits himself to the *ming* as destiny" just means to "resign" oneself to it and let it be.

After the quotation of Confucian thoughts, here come the doctrines both of Taoism and Buddhism:

> "*To say them respectively, they are two, and to mention them together, they are actually one; and they contain the principle therein. Hence, shen(神spirit, mind, soul or consciousness) does not depart from qi (氣), and qi does not depart from shen; where the shen and qi in my body are combined, the xing and*

ming of my body are manifested. Xing does not depart from ming, and ming does not depart from xing; where the xing and ming in my body are combined, the xing and ming prior to the xing and ming in my body are revealed. The xing and ming prior to the xing and ming in my body are the true xing and ming of mine, and the true xing and ming are just the true xing and ming both of the Heaven and the Earth, and the true xing and ming of voidness. Therefore, the greatly virtuous adhere to the principle of precepts, concentration and wisdom （聖賢持戒、定、慧）*and empty their mind, cultivates jing (the physical basis of vitality), qi and shen to preserve their bodies*（鍊精、氣、神以保其身）*. With their bodies preserved, their ming will have a permanent and firm foundation; with their minds emptied, their nature will have a permanent enlightened form. As the nature is always enlightened, there would be no coming and going; as the ming has a permanent and firm foundation, there would be no life and death. Moreover, what die and pass away are merely physical bodies, but the true xing and ming of mine equate day with night, match up with the Heaven and the Earth, and remain the same all the time, when did they ever diminish or vanish?"*

And also, there is a poem whose major idea is like this:

The dual cultivation of xing and ming is the right learning of cultivation, （性命双修是的傳）
Which is abstruse, profound and indescribable.
（冥冥杳杳又玄玄）
Who knows that the thing-in-itself has no life and death?
（誰知本體無生死）
And what causes the phenomenon of life and death in the world?
（死死生生孰使然）

Li Hongzhi cannot understand the above-mentioned profound theory, of course, and he has simply plagiarized the expression of "dual cultivation of *xing* and *ming*" for his own use. In essence, when he propagates his so-called "cultivation of nature", he is actually demanding his disciples to have superstition about his "cosmic law", and when he advocates his so-called "cultivation of *ming*", he is simply asking his disciples to industriously practice his five sets of "Falun Gongfa".

Notes:

1. *Zhuan Falun*, pp. 219 & 220.
2. Mencius demonstrated the "man is good in nature" with "The feeling of commiseration implies the principle of benevolence; that of shame and dislike, the principle of righteousness; that of reverence and respect, the principle of propriety; and that of approving and disapproving, the principle of intelligence. They belong to all men"; this is great argumentation of moral philosophy. See Gaozi, First Part, the *Writings of Mencius*（孟子・告子上）.
3. Mou Zongsan, *On the Summum Bonum*（牟宗三：圓善論）, pp. 142-144. Taiwan: Student Book Co., Ltd., 1996, 2nd print run.

What Is "Arhat"?

Li Hongzhi likes to mention "the fruit of *luohan(羅漢)* (arhat)" so as to solicit his "disciples" to practice his "Fofa". In fact, he does not seem to know what "arhat" is. He says,

> *"As a man reaches the stage of practice of supermundane dharma, he will have reached the level of the practice of the fruit of arhats, and that is the primary fruit of arhats. At that time, he can be viewed as a Buddha, actually you are practicing in the form of a Buddha. Arhats can be divided as primary arhats, right fruit of arhats and grand arhats. The disparities between each level are very huge…"* ①

This passage is a nonsense based on sciolism.

"Arhat" is a Sanskrit word, and its transliteration in Chinese is *"aluohan"* （阿羅漢）, shortened as *"luohan"* （羅漢）. This Buddhist term has several meanings, but in the scriptures of Chinese Buddhism, it usually refers to the highest status of fruits (the greatly virtuous who has successfully practiced Buddhism) in the Hinayana practice. Just because he has been at the highest status of fruits, there are no such differences as the "primary", "right fruit" or "grand".

The practice of Hinayana Buddhism has four stages:

1. Srota-apanna: It means "to enter the rank", that is, one can be viewed as has ranked among saints only if he has reached this stage.
2. Sakrdagamin: It means "one single round of coming and passing away"; one who has reached this second stage needs to be born as a human being only once, and then he will be able to enter the realm of unconditioned nirvana.
3. Anagamin: It means "not to return". When he reaches this third stage, one will not be confused by the falseness of this world anymore, that is, he will have eliminated all the defilements of the desire realm.
4. Arhat: It means "ought to receive offerings", that is, the greatly virtuous that deserves people's devotion and worship. This is the highest realm of Hinayana Buddhism, the highest status of fruit that has eliminated all contaminations.

The arhat in Hinayana Buddhism has reached the realm of a saint (the total elimination of contaminations), but he is a "man who takes care only of himself" anyhow, and is different from the level of bodhisattva in Mahayana. In Chinese, "*pusa*" (菩薩) is the shorten term for "*puti saduo*" (菩提薩埵), which is the transliteration of a Sanskrit word "Bodhisattva". Originally, this term meant to "enlighten sentient beings", and it was designed to help others to get free of vexation and sufferings. This is the most important difference between a bodhisattva and an arhat. Moreover, arhat itself is the highest status of fruit already, and cannot be graded anymore, but bodhisattvas can be divided into ten levels. So, it is acceptable to say "grand bodhisattva" and "junior bodhisattva".②

Meanwhile, an arhat is absolutely inferior to a "Buddha" in terms of their statuses although the former is the highest fruit in Hinayana Buddhism. The Chinese character "*fo*"(佛) is a transliteration of the Sanskrit word "Boddha", which means "an enlightened person". According to a consensus of all Buddhist sects, however, "Buddha" is the highest achievement of Buddhist practice, and this degree has three characteristics: 1. Self-enlightenment; 2. The enlightenment of others; and 3. The consummate enlightenment. An arhat is a man who has merely enlightened himself. In comparison, the enlightenment of others is the distinctive characteristic of a bodhisattva, that is, to commit the merits of rescuing all the other living beings. That is not the target of an arhat. Furthermore, the "consummate enlightenment" is even further beyond the expectation of arhat. So, Li is wrong when he says that "an arhat can be viewed as a Buddha".

Obviously, Li does not know the above-mentioned differences, and he simply snatches the term "arhat" to talk nonsense. Now that he is fond of teaching others, how can he be so imprecise? He must keep in mind that a teacher who misteaches students would fall into the Avichi Hells (hells of ceaseless sufferings, the worst among all hells).

Notes:
1. *Falun Dafa Interpretation*, p. 10.
2. As for the theory about the practice of a bodhisattva and the detail of related stages, see the author's *Selection of Buddhist Doctrines*, Chapter 7.

The Issue of Precepts

Buddhist scriptures are divided into the three parts of Sutra-pitaka (scriptures about doctrines), Vinayapitaka (precepts established by Sakyamuni) and Abhidharma Pitika (explanatory treatises). Here, "sutras" are the doctrines preached by Sakyamuni himself, "precepts" are the precepts of Buddhism, and "explanatory treatises" are the works by Buddhist masters except Sakyamuni. Most "explanatory treatises" are the explanations for "sutras", and some are those for "precepts".

So to speak, "sutras" have represented the thoughts of Buddhism, and "precepts" regulate the criteria of Buddhism. Thoughts and criteria are like the wings of a bird, they are equally important to the development of Buddhism over the two thousand years in the past, and both of them are indispensable.

Both sutras and precepts are teachings from the Buddha, but the Buddha did not leave any writings in his propaganda over 40 years. About half a year after his passing, five hundred disciples assembled, putting down the Buddha's teachings in writing. That was the famous "First Council". The compilation as a result of this council was divided into two parts, one of which was "sutras", and the other was just "precepts". Afterwards, similar "councils" were held for several times.①

The above-mentioned are largely the source of primitive Buddhist sutras and precepts, and are familiar to anyone who knows even a little history of Buddhism. Li Hongzhi, however, seems not to have really read through a copy of the history of Buddhism, so he talks nonsense before he knows even nothing of the simplest Buddhist knowledge. It does not matter if he merely talks nonsense for himself, but the point is that he calls his nonsense "scriptures" to teach his "disciples", is he not committing evil karma when he misteaches people as such?

Now, let's quote two passages from his writings. He says,

> *"There were no Buddhist scriptures or writings in Sakyamuni's days. After Sakyamuni died, people of later generations recollected Sakyamuni's words, collated and put them down in writings as scriptures. Sakyamuni had established many regulations about practice and viewed them as precepts when he lived, and these things have come down in writing."* ②

Li Hongzhi is wrong when he alleges that Sakyamuni left no scriptures, but precepts in writing when he lived. Again he says,

> *"Sakyamuni left only precepts at that time, and he did not leave any writings when he lived. In the course of practice in his late years, Sakyamuni established many precepts so that people could continue their practice and cultivation and make achievements in such practice. But today we have no such things. As a matter of fact, the kernel thing that Sakyamuni left is only precepts."* ③

This passage is incorrect in the following four points:

1. Sakyamuni did not leave "mere precepts."

As it is described above, Sakyamuni did not leave any writings when he propagated Buddhism. But sooner than half a year after his passing, his disciples who had directly followed him assembled to "compile" in strict procedures the teachings and "Pratimoksa" that the Buddha had taught himself. The former turned out to be the extant four kinds of "*Agama Sutras*", and the latter are just Buddhist precepts. The *Agama Sutras* are the most primitive Buddhist doctrines, and the "precepts" are the code of conduct of Buddhist monastics (the sangha).

2. Precepts were not established only in the Buddha's late years.

In the earliest stage of the Buddha's propaganda, the disciples were in small numbers and thus had similarly good characters, so there was no need of precepts. Twelve years later, a disciple whose name was Sudina committed a lewd activity, hence the first precept was established. Afterwards, as the numbers of disciples increased, various bad things constantly happened, so the Buddha had to establish new precepts where there were newly committed wrongdoings. In a word, Sakyamuni propagated Buddhism for more than 40 years (some people argue that it was 45 years, some others 49 years) until his passing at 80. So, no matter how it is calculated, it is absolutely not that he began to establish disciplines in his late years; the case should be that the Buddha began to establish precepts in his forties.

3. The purpose of the establishment of such precepts was not limited to "that people could continue their practice and cultivation."

All kinds of scriptures about precepts clearly record that the Buddha had as many as ten purposes when he established precepts,④ and they are absolutely not so simple as Li has described. Moreover, the Buddha did not establish all these precepts at one single time; instead, he established "new precepts where there were newly committed wrongdoings"—He established a precept only when someone committed something wrong. Such situation continued until the passing of the Buddha, and as many as two or three hundred precepts were established (According to the *Vinaya of the Four Categories* (四分律), there are 250 precepts for male monastics, and 348 for female ones).

4. The most important things that Sakyamuni left are not limited to precepts.

As it is mentioned above, several months later after the Buddha's passing, his disciples assembled to compile the four *Agama Sutras* and precepts. Precepts are the code of conduct, and are important to the survival and development of Buddhism, so the Buddha left his last words at his passing, "Where the Vinaya last long, the Buddhism lasts long." But as a religion or philosophical thought, the true kernel is the doctrinal part anyhow, for without doctrines, the code of conduct will become meaningless. The doctrines of Buddhism have been called "the teachings of edification"—teachings to edify the minds of human beings, and its precepts have been called "the teachings of practices"—the code of conduct. The doctrines and precepts left by the Buddha are indispensable. Therefore, Li is wrong when he alleges that "the kernel thing that Sakyamuni left is only precepts".

Notes:

1. It is said that the "compilation" of Buddhism happened four times, but that at the first and the second times is the most important. The first compilation took place several months later after the Buddha's passing, and the second one was conducted a hundred years later because of the disputes about some precepts between different sects. See the author's *Fundamentals of Precept Studies*, p. 57, Taiwan Lao Ku Culture Foundation Inc.; the *Buddhist Precepts Studies*, p. 44, Beijing Religious Culture Publishing House, 2003, 3rd print run.

2. *Falun Dafa Interpretation*, p. 28.

3. Ibid, p. 126.

4. See the author's *Fundamentals of Precept Studies*, p. 50, Taiwan Lao Ku Culture Foundation Inc.; the *Buddhist Precepts Studies*, p. 39, Beijing Religious Culture Publishing House, 2003, 3rd print run. This issue is very complicated and it is inconvenient to expatiate here, those who are interested can consult these two books.

What Are "Sanqian Daqian Shijie" (One Billion Worlds)?

The "*sanqian daqian shijie*"三千大千世界 (one billion worlds) is a term that the ancient Indians called the whole universe, and it was not a theory established by the Buddha; it is true that some Buddhist scriptures frequently make use of it, but they are merely borrowing the traditional parlance of ancient India. Li Hongzhi tells his "disciples" as such without making clear the source of this term:

> "*Sakyamuni had also propagated the theory of 'sanqian daqian shijie'.*"①

In what scripture did Sakyamuni ever propagate the "theory of *sanqian daqian shijie*"? Li Hongzhi often makes such mistakes as to call white black, put the boot on the wrong leg, misunderstand classical texts and take the ancient people's words too literally, that is because he has read too few books and is thus too superficial. One deserves sympathy if he has not read enough books and is thus unlearned because of various limitations, but a man like Li Hongzhi, who professes that he did not go to college because he *"cannot form various concepts, theorems, definitions, laws, theories or various regulated thing"* (See the 6th section above, "Li Hongzhi's Fundamental Deviation"), can have no excuse for his ignorance.

What is more unforgivable is that Li Hongzhi surprisingly castigates some scholars of religion who have criticized him, *"Some ruffians living on religions even cannot clearly explain these nouns, are they qualified to criticize the Falun Dafa?"* (See the *Essentials for Further Advances*, p. 148) This remark is suitable merely for Li Hongzhi himself in turn. Now, let's make use of the concept "one billion worlds" to test whether Li's concepts are clear or not.

The Meaning of "Sanqian Daqian Shijie" (One Billion Worlds)

Li continues,

"He (Sakyamuni) said in this universe of ours, in this Galaxy of ours, there were three thousand planets which were inhabited with physical bodies like those of us human beings."

That is peculiar; when did the Buddha mentioned the word "universe"? Had the Indians 2,500 years ago know there is a "Galaxy"? The expression "three thousand planets" further indicates that Li does not know what the expression *sanqian daqian shijie* (one billion worlds) means.

Actually, in the ancient India, there was no such word as "universe", they knew only the "world" (See details in next section). According to the ancient Indians, the so-called "world" is centered around Mount Sumeru. Around Mount Sumeru there are four enormous continents; beyond the four continents are nine mountains and eight oceans; that is the world where we human beings live. That is one world. A thousand worlds like this constitute a larger world, which is called "One Thousand Worlds". A thousand larger worlds together constitute a "One Million Worlds", and likewise, a thousand "One Million Worlds" together are a "One Billion Worlds". This "One Billion Worlds" is as large as the fourth meditation heaven（四禪天）, and comes into being and is destructed synchronically as the latter does. This "One Billion Worlds" is one billion times as many as the world inhabited by us, and that is why it is called "One Billion Worlds". It is absolutely not "three thousand small worlds", let alone "three thousand planets" as Li drivels about. Buddhist scriptures borrow this term to describe the sphere of influence of one Buddha's edification, alluding to the "vastness of territories under one Buddha".②

The above proves that Li has begun to blather on before he knows little about the meaning of the expression "One Billion Worlds".

Li's Ignorance of the Huayan School（華嚴宗）

After the quotation above, Li utters even stranger remarks:

"He (Sakyamuni) had also remarked that a piece of sand contained such a 'sanqian daqian shijie'. One piece of sand was just like a universe, which contained men of wisdom like us, planets like ours, and mountains and rivers. It sounds unbelievable! If it were true, you just think about it, does this 'sanqian daqian shijie' still contain sands? Does any piece of sand in it still contain a 'sanqian daqian shijie'? Do such new 'sanqian daqian shijie' still contain sands? And does a piece of sand in such new 'sanqian daqian shijie' contain another set of 'sanqian daqian shijie'? So, a person at the level of the Thus-Come is unable to see its boundaries."

Here, the author has a question to ask the Master: In what scripture did Sakyamuni make such remark as "a piece of sand contained such a *sanqian daqian shijie*"? Actually, it is the Huayan School of Chinese Buddhism that made similar remarks, which are the analytic description of the doctrine of "dependent origination caused by dharma". For example, the Huayan School has such weird remarks such as "a small dust contains the whole world"（一微塵攝全法界）, "the whole world is contained in a small dust"（全法界遍一微塵）, "one is just many"（一即多）, "many are merely one"（多即一）, "one flower equates to one world, and one leaf reflects one Thus-Come"（一花一世界，一葉一如來） and so forth. But these remarks are merely the analysis of the relationships of mutual dependent origination of all things in the world, and they do not point at any particular things existing in times and space; they are merely poetic metaphors, but not the explanation of any physical existences. If one understands these weird expressions as Li Hongzhi does, who surprisingly says that "One piece of sand was just like a universe, which contained men of wisdom like us, the planets like ours, and mountains and rivers", that is, if one views them as the explanation of particular objects in the sense of space physics, it would be too ridiculous. That proves his total ignorance of the doctrines of the Huayan School.

The expatiation on the doctrine of "dependent origination of realm of phenomena" is the most important contribution that the Huayan School has made. "Dependent origination" (緣起) is the most basic theory of Buddhism, and it holds that nothing in the world has its own nature, and that all things arise dependently (As for the meaning of self-nature, see Section 8 above, "Who Is Plagiarizing Dharma"). Sakyamuni was a crown prince, but was afflicted with the vexation of man caused by birth, senility, illness and death, so he became a monastic to seek for solutions of such afflictions. He failed after 6 years austerity. At last, he sat in meditation under a bodhi tree. Meditating for 49 days at one breath, he suddenly became enlightened. Then, what did the Buddha realize? He realized the principle of "dependent origination" of afflictions of human life, which is called "twelve limbs of dependent origination".③ That is the source of theory about dependent origination, the creation made by the Buddha.

However, what is the dependent origination itself? This is a very complicated question, and the research continued by later generations led to four theories about dependent origination, now they are briefly recounted as follows:

1. Dependent origination caused by karmas (業感緣起): A theory about dependent origination in Hinayana Buddhism. A man commits many wrongdoings (karma) because of "ignorance" and thus produces various afflictions (sufferings, literally "*ku*" in Chinese). Suffering from life and death, the man experiences transmigration again and again,

then causes new confusion and produces new karma, and is plunged into such affliction once again. In this way, the "delusion", "karma" and "suffering" form a vicious circle and continue endlessly. The origination, extinguishment, changes and evolution of all things in the field of phenomena can be explained, together with the afflicting life and death of a man. That is the main points of the theory about dependent origination in Hinayana Buddhism.

2. Dependent origination based on alaya consciousness (阿賴耶缘起): The theory about dependent origination in the Consciousness-Only School. The 8th level of a man's consciousness is called alaya consciousness, which contains the seeds of all dharma; it is the source of a man's life and objective things. The very "dependent origination" of things and a man's behaviors depend upon alaya consciousness, so it is called the dependent origination based on alaya consciousness.

3. Dependent origination based on true-thusness (真如缘起also known as dependent origination based on tathagatagarbha): This is a theory in the tathagatagarbha system of Buddhism. Its main point is like this: the original spirit of us as human beings is called "tathagatagarbha", and it can be divided into two parts: the gate of true-thusness and the gate of origination and extinction. The dependent origination is rooted in the "gate of origination and extinction", while the very reason why a man can practice the doctrines of Buddhism and make the achievements of bodhisattva and Buddha rests in the "gate of true-thusness".

4. Dependent Origination of Realm of Phenomena (法界缘起): The very theory of the Huayan School, which is about dependent origination based on the realm of phenomena. This kind of theory about dependent origination is different from the former

three kinds. The first kind is from the point of view of the practical aspect of a human life, that is, it talks about the beingness of dependent origination from the causality of "confusion", "karma" and "suffering", the second and the third kinds explore reversely the very source of dependent origination. This kind of theory about dependent origination, however, explains the mutual relationships of "perfect penetration without obstruction" (圓融無礙) between all things in the universe. Such relationships are not any description at a practical level; rather, it is a realm that the Buddha realized and demonstrated in his extremely deep meditation, in other words, it deals with the doctrine about dependent origination from the point of view of ideal value. As for how to achieve the relation of "perfect penetration without obstruction", it is based on such weird logic as "mutual identity" (相即), "mutual entry" (相入) and "mutual containment" (相攝), a special structure established by the masters of the Huayan School. For example, the sentence that "one dust can contain the whole universe" as mentioned above is a description about such relation of "perfect penetration without obstruction".④

Overall, it is uneasy to largely learn about the "theory about dependent origination" in Buddhism already, and it is even more difficult to really understand the "dependent origination based on the realm of phenomena" of the Huayan School. Li Hongzhi is not learned enough to understand the theory of the Huayan School, of course, so it is natural that he thus blathers by taking words literally. But what matters is that he pretends to be knowledgeable and positions himself as above the level of Sakyamuni, readily indoctrinating others and arrogantly calling his nonsense "scriptures"; that is what should be seriously denounced.

Advice to Li Hongzhi

Judging from Li's various misunderstandings about Buddhism, including his fabricating the history of Buddhism, his misconstruing such basic Buddhist doctrines as "emptiness", "non-duality dharma-gate", "One Billion Worlds", "dependent origination" and so on, and his denouncing the Chan School, we can come to a conclusion that he actually does not understand Buddhism. Most people in the world do not understand Buddhism, so it does not matter if one does not know Buddhism well; but it is unacceptable that Li Hongzhi castigates, denies and rails against Buddhism although he knows little about it.

Li does so to establish his position as a "supreme hierarch", of course. A man who is ambitious is respectable, and it is all right that Li has such an ambition as to initiate a new religion. But he is wrong as he does not realize his ambition in a proper way: He castigates Buddhism and even plagiarizes many Buddhist terms as his banner although he does not understand Buddhism. So to speak, such misconduct is so ludicrous that it is really unforgivable.

Taking advantage of this occasion, the author would like to offer three pieces of advice to Li:

First, study Buddhism modestly.

Buddhism involves knowledge both widely and profoundly; to understand Buddhism will be naturally very helpful to human life. Xiong Shili (熊十力), a great Neo-Confucian of modern times, uttered a wonderful remark when he estimated the thought of Buddhism, which deserves our quotation and reference:

"I have studied all the doctrines of Buddhism in general. In my opinion, it has three surpassing points in all ages:

1. It penetrates the confusion and contamination in human life; people can be thus taught to return to themselves. In our opinion, no other thoughts have perceived the confusion or contamination in human life more profoundly than Buddhism ever since the beginning of the Heaven and the Earth. (Original Note: Many thinkers both at home and abroad have pointed out the defects of human beings, but they held a callous attitude when they did so; moreover, they did so with worldly wisdom at the level of superficial knowledge and understanding, not from the bottom of a heart with great mercy, let alone with width and profundity. This cannot be easily articulated from a worldly point.)

2. Buddhist works have described the one true dharmadhatu which is characterized with emptiness, tranquility, purity and reality; and it is far from all perversion, illusion or groundless remarks, revealing peerless dignity. It would impress Yan Yuan（顏子）, *a greatly virtuous only next to Confucius, with such superiority that there were no way to match up with, and we can hardly eulogize it enough. It would be an extreme pity if one does not comprehend it in his life.*

3. Buddhist books are really unmatchable both at home and abroad in all ages in terms of its denial of the knowledge based on street wisdom or emotions. It is true that both Laotze and Zhuangzi opposed such knowledge, but judging from their remarks, they still did not reach the highest realm, and were inferior to Buddhism, of course. The Western philosophers have largely been limited to the speculative philosophy, and are inferior even to Laotze and Zhuangzi. Confucius had an enough ambit, but he was reluctant to develop toward this direction. So, Buddhism is indispensable. As for the learning of Buddhism, we should have an eye at its aspects of grandeur and profundity. Most people indulging in Buddhism in China have been famous scholars, but fond of talking about its wonder and abstruseness, they all fell into ambiguity and confusion, doing harm to the circle of thinkers for long; they have not been really benefited from Buddhism."⑤

The doctrines of Buddhism are so thorough, solemn, wonderful and profound that it is natural that a street man finds it very difficult to learn its rudiments. But Li has such an ambition that he is certainly different from a street man, so he should have tried to understand Buddhism well regardless of difficulties.

Second, endeavor to learn about the learning of Chinese Buddhism.

After it was introduced into China, Buddhism was gradually accepted and nationalized; five hundred years later, the Chinese people finally established with their wisdom the Mahayana Buddhism fully with Chinese characteristics: the Tiantai School, the Huayan School, the Chan School and the Vinaya School.⑥ In particular, the Tiantai School is good at the philosophy of mind, the Huayan School is conspicuous of it profound and enormous theoretic system, the Chan School has its strength in its various flexible teaching methods to achieve the goal of "enlightening the mind and seeing through the nature", and the Vinaya School has elevated the code of conduct up to the level of "Jurisprudence of Buddhism". Liang Qichao （梁啟超）once praised it as such,

> *"So great China is! It can develop any foreign learning and make the latter feature a Chinese characteristic once it accepts it. I have seen it in math, and I have also seen it in Buddhism; Chinese Buddhism is the Buddhism of China, not purely the Buddhism in an Indian style…I myself am convinced that the China tens of years later will certainly integrate both the Chinese and Western learning to produce a new kind of civilization of China. I wish for it from the bottom of my heart, and I eulogize the great achievements of the great monastics of the Sui and Tang dynasties to urge the youth of our days."*⑦

As mentioned above, Li has not only misunderstood the principle that Buddhism has been constantly developed, but also knows nothing about the great achievements of Chinese Buddhism; if Li is really aspirant, Liang's remark as is quoted above should be inspiring to him.

Thirdly, show proper respect to worldly truths.

"Worldly truths" are just all the principles and knowledge in a "society of mediocre people" in Li's term, including the proprieties and etiquette of people when they mix with each other, the knowledge of all trades and so forth. What is opposite to "worldly truths" is the "ultimate truth" (the primary truths), i.e., the truths transcendent over the secular world, and the "cosmic law" that Li professes to propagate just belongs to this field. What is the relation between these kinds of truths? We can explain it by quoting three verses from An Examination of Four Truths in Nagarjuna's *Madhyamika-sastra* (龍樹：中論・觀四諦品)：

All Buddhas propagate Buddhist doctrines,
In the light of two kinds of truths. （諸佛依二諦，為眾生說法）
One is the worldly truths, （一以世俗諦）
And the other is primary truths. （二第一義諦）

If he is unable to know, （若人不能知）
The difference between the two kinds of truths, （分別於二諦）
He will fail to understand, （則於深佛法，不知真實義）
The true meaning of extremely profound Buddhist doctrines.

He who does not follow worldly truths,
Will be unable to know the primary truths; （若不依俗諦，不得第一義）
He who fails to know the primary truths,
Will be unable to achieve nirvana. （不得第一義，則不得涅槃）

In these three verses, Nagarjuna clearly pointed out that there were two kinds of truths in the world, both of which were the doctrines that Buddhism has used to edify living beings. We must tell them apart; meantime, we must learn about the relation between these two. The so-called "worldly truths" are just the rules as common sense based on reason (for example, the knowledge of all disciplines, the law of logic, the rules of languages and words, and so forth), and a person can realize the "primary truths" (the truths transcendent over worldly knowledge) at a higher level only through the understanding of "worldly truths". The other way round, there would be no way to the higher realm if confused with things in the society of mediocre people (He who does not follow worldly truths will be unable to know the first truth).

The relation between these two kinds of truths can also be explained with two famous sentences in the *Heart Sutra* (心經) : "*se* is just *kong*" （色即是空）and "*kong* is just *se*" （空即是色）. Here, "*se*" refers to "physical forms", i.e., things within the category of matter, and it belongs to the worldly truth. "*Kong*" refers to the realm transcending the secular world, belonging to the ultimate truth. Hence, the first sentence that "*se* is just *kong*" teaches people not cling to worldly things; instead, they should transcend the worldly things to reach the higher realm of the ultimate truth. The second sentence that "*kong* is just *se*" is even more abstruse, and it intends that it is not that there is a world named "emptiness" outside the worldly existences, and that the ultimate truth (emptiness) must depend upon world truths. Concretely, we must know the society of common people and do well the things in such a society before we transcend it. This is very important to those who practice Buddhism. It is fraudulent or insane to attempt the transcendence over a secular society without understanding it first. When he rebukes juniors who are unfamiliar with secular matters, Master Nan Huaijin often says like this, "How can you learn to practice Buddhism now that you have not learned how to conduct yourself well?" This remark is very profound.

As it is shown in the related analysis in all sections of this book, Li is so limited and superficial in his cognizing "world truths" that he is muddleheaded with them. But he tries to justify all his ignorance with such excuse as "the Dafa that I propagate is not a thing of the society of mediocre people". Is he intending to deceive or is he insane on earth? Li himself should have more self-reflection.

Notes:
1. *Zhuan Falun*, pp. 68-69. The quotations infra are the same as this one, so no separate notes will be given anymore.
2. As for the meaning of "One Billion Worlds", see Wu Rujun, author and compiler, *Buddhist Thoughts Dictionary.* Taiwan Commercial Press, 1994, 2nd print run.
3. For the detail of "twelve limbs of dependent origination", see the author's *Selection of Buddhist Doctrines*, Chapter Four, Section One.
4. The theory of the Huayan School is difficult to understand, and common works on this subject merely parrot it in the main. For the real understanding of its abstruse meaning, it is advisable to peruse the following works:

Mou Zongsan, *Buddha-Nature and Prajna*, （牟宗三: 佛性與般若）Vol. 1, Chapter 6. Taiwan Student Book Co., Ltd., 1993, 5th edition.

Tang Junyi, *Research on the Origin of Tao* in the *Research on the Origin of Chinese Philosophy* （唐君毅: 中國哲學原論・原道篇）Vol. 3, Chapters 11, 12 & 13, Taiwan Student Book Co., Ltd., 2000, 3rd edition.

Fang Dongmei, *The Philosophy of the Huayan School*, （方東美: 華嚴宗哲學） Taiwan Liming Culture Co., Ltd., 1983, 2nd edition.

Wu Rujun, *Modern Interpretations of Chinese Buddhism*, （吳汝鈞: 中國佛學的現代詮釋）Chapter 8. Taipei, China Social Sciences Press, 1998, 2nd print run.

5. See Xiong Shili, *New Consciousness-only Theory*, （熊十力：新唯識論）Vol. Two, pp. 613-614. Taipei Mingwen Bookstore Co., Ltd, 1991. The quotation is an extract, and is punctuated by the author. Xiong Shili (1885—1968) was a great philosopher in modern China recognized by academia as had "a huge scale and unique insight". He once taught in the Peking University. He started with Buddhism and intended for Confucianism, leaving writings such as the *New Consciousness-only Theory*, the *Essentials for Reading the Classics*（讀經示要）and the *Research on the Origin of Confucianism*（原儒）, which have been profoundly influential. He showed the unyielding character of a Confucian in his late years, and that especially deserves to be a paragon for later generations.

6. In general, the Mahayana Buddhism of China is divided into 8 sects. In particular, the Three-treatise School, the Consciousness-only Sect and the Esoteric Buddhism directly came from India, and have fewer Chinese characteristics; in addition, the Pure Land School is mostly from India, and belongs to the dharma-gate of pure practice. Hence, when people mention the Buddhist sects with Chinese characteristics, they allude merely to four sects. As for the detail of Chinese Buddhism, see the author's *Selection of Buddhist Doctrines*, Chapters 9 & 10.

7. *The Collected Works of Liang Qichao*（梁啟超集）, pp. 63-64. Beijing: China Social Sciences Press, 1995, 1st edition.

The Attachment to and Castigation against Greatly Virtuous Sages

Li Hongzhi has a bad tactic, that is, he attaches himself to some greatly virtuous sages both at home and abroad to elevate himself on the one hand, and feigns remarks that such sages have never said or events that they have never done to criticize them so as to prove he is superior to those sages. Such a method of attachment and denouncement is most frequently used on the Thus-Come Buddha. For example,

> *"Sakyamuni said in his late years, 'It can be indefinitely large so that it has no edge, and it can be indefinitely small so that it has no internal room.' What does it mean? At the level of the Thus-Come, one cannot see the edge of the universe from the point of view of hugeness, and cannot see the smallest particle of material from the point of view of smallness. That is why he said 'It can be indefinitely large so that it has no edge, and it can be indefinitely small so that it has no internal room'."*

This is nonsense. In what scripture did the Thus-Come ever say such a sentence as "It can be indefinitely large so that it has no edge, and it can be indefinitely small so that it has no internal room"? Even if the Thus-Come had really said so, he absolutely would not mean that "one cannot see the edge of the universe from the point of view of hugeness, and cannot see the smallest particle of material from the point of view of smallness".

Such a sentence as "it can be indefinitely large so that it has no edge, and it can be indefinitely small so that it has no internal room" can be frequently seen in traditional Confucian and Taoist scriptures of China, and it actually intended for weakening the ideas of hugeness and smallness. In addition, it was also used to describe political authority, for example, when a political leader was mentioned who united all possible forces to expand the foundation of his power, it can be said that "it can be indefinitely large so that it has no edge"; but when his power was threatened or endangered, he would sacrifice even his closest relatives, and that is "it can be indefinitely small so that it has no internal room". Many Buddhist works during the Sui and Tang dynasties often quoted this sentence, too; but in most cases, it was used to describe the consciousness and mind of human beings, suggesting that the power of mind was unlimited. But no matter what it intended, that sentence does not mean what Li has mentioned, and what is more, Li has attributed it to a wrong person completely on purpose. Then, why did he do so? Let's have a look at the following:

> *"People may ask how huge the universe may be, now I tell you this universe does have its edge, but at the level of the Thus-Come, people all view it as endless, or infinitely huge."* ①

That is Li Hongzhi's purpose: "I am superior to the Buddha!" The Buddha had reached only "the level of the Thus-come" and was thus unable to see the edge of the universe, but I can see the edge of the universe. In other words, Sakyamuni was able to see only part of the universe, but I, Master Li, have seen the whole universe. Doubtlessly I am much superior to the Buddha.

Not replying to Fourteen Questions

As a matter of fact, as for the question whether the universe has an edge or not, the Buddha had never given such explicit answer as "yes" or "no" as Li has fabricated; instead, he took an attitude of "the great sage's reticence", giving no answer to this question. This matter has been explicitly recorded in Buddhist sutras.

As Sakyamuni was still living in this world, some heretics once made 14 difficult questions to the Buddha, but the latter refused to answer. That is the famous case of "not replying to fourteen difficult questions" (also known as "fourteen indeterminate questions") in Buddhism.② These 14 questions are as follows:

1. *Is the world of "eternality"?*
2. *Is the world of "non-eternality"?*
3. *Is the world of "eternality and meanwhile non-eternality"?*
4. *Is the world of "non-eternality" and meanwhile not of "non-eternality"?*
5. *Is the world of "limit"?*
6. *Is the world of "non-limit"?*
7. *Is the world of "limit" and meanwhile of "non-limit"?*
8. *Is the world of "non-limit" and meanwhile not of "non-limit"?*
9. *Is the Thus-Come an "existence" after his passing?*
10. *Is the Thus-Come "non-existence" after his passing?*
11. *Is the Thus-Come "existence" and meanwhile "non-existence" after his passing?*
12. *Is the Thus-Come "non-existence" and meanwhile not "non-existence" after his passing?*
13. *Is self "identical" with a physical body?*
14. *Is self "different" from a physical body?*

Why did Sakyamuni not answer the above-mentioned 14 questions? What Sakyamuni was deeply concerned with was how to get rid of the endless affliction and vexation of human life in reality, but those speculative questions belong to the field of metaphysics, and not the concerns of Buddhism, that was why he did not reply to them.

This attitude of the Buddha is somewhat like that of Confucius, a greatly virtuous sage of China. Confucius cared about nothing but the issue of "benevolence" (仁), which belongs to ethnics, and he would put no single word in such questions as "prodigies, force, disorders and gods" (子不語怪、力、亂、神) which are beyond this sphere. When a disciple consulted him about matters after a man's death, Confucius answered him as such, "How could you know death as you do not know life thoroughly?" (Xianjin, the *Analects of Confucius*) This is a very brilliant reply. "To acknowledge what is known as known and what is not known as not known is knowledge." (Weizheng, the *Analects of Confucius*) It was not because of elusion or superficiality that both the Buddha and Confucius refused to reply to some questions, but that a truly virtuous sage had his sense of propriety and modesty. Only those who profess to be learned and think themselves omnipotent are truly superficial.

As it is analyzed in Section 13 titled "What Is Non-duality Dharma-gate" above, some abstruse philosophical or religious issues are beyond man's intelligence, and belong to the level that "The path of language is cut off, and the ubiety of mental formations vanishes", that is, they are indescribable; a man of great virtues can only remain "tacit" to respond to a question at this level. Obviously Li has not reached such level of abstruseness, that is why he dare casually criticize the Chan School as "there is no dharma to propagate" and "they cannot hit the point whenever they propagate", and that is why he dare think himself even superior to the Buddha.

He Talks Madly about the Universe

Li Hongzhi professes that his "Dafa" is the highest dharma in the universe, and that he is superior to the Buddha, let alone Confucius, Jesus and Laotze. So, he frequently talks about science ranging from neutrins to multiple universe spaces, as if he were an omniscient and omnipotent Jehovah.

Now, let's have a look at his two passages about the universe:

"The Falun world is a world unit of this universe of ours at a very high level. The universe is very enormous. Some are new trainees, so I have to be conservative in my speech, for I am afraid they cannot accept such ideas. In this enormous universe of ours,

there are numberless smaller universes. Mankind lives in one of these smaller universe, and in these smaller universes there are numberless Galaxies. The Buddha, who was at the level of the Thus-Come, was unable to see the edge of a smaller universe; the larger universe is so large that a man was not allowed to know its size in the past. It is really too enormous."③

The main point of this passage is that what I Li Hongzhi see is the whole large universe, that the large universe contains numberless smaller universes, and that human beings simply live in one of such smaller universes. In the past, the Thus-Come Buddha was at a low level, so he knew only one universe, and his ability was so limited that he was not able to see the edge of this smaller universe.

Li continues,

"The universe does have its edge, but let's not talk about such a thing. This edge is too far; at the level of the Thus-Come, the edge of the universe refers to the edge of a smaller universe. But this smaller universe seems to be endless and unfathomable even to the Thus-Come Buddha, let alone human beings; it is very very enormous."④

This passage more clearly stresses that the Buddha was not able to see the whole of even a smaller universe, (no wonder that he said the universe was endless), but what I Li Hongzhi sees is the enormous large universe which contains numberless universes and galaxies; what is more, I have even seen the edge of the large universe! That proves my insight is much deeper than that of the Buddha.

Li's remarks as such cannot but make others suspect whether he is insane. Or otherwise, how can he be so arrogant and boastful? Such a question as "whether the universe has an edge or not" was just what even the Buddha dare not answer, and so it is with the greatest scientists such as Albert Einstein and Stephen Hawking.⑤

By the way, the term *"yuzhou"* (宇宙universe) was not invented by Buddhism; instead, it is a traditional Chinese term. As early as before the Qin and Han dynasties, there had been the term *"yuzhou"*, as well as a clear explanation that "the expanse in four directions and above and below are called *yu*, and the times from the ancient to the present are called *zhou*";⑥ so, the term *"yuzhou"* just refers to space and time. After the modern western philosophy and science were introduced into China, the terms *"yuzhou"* (the universe) and *"yuzhoulun"* (cosmology) began to become popular in Chinese language.

Actually, Buddhist did not employ the term *"yuzhou"*, and it was less possible that Sakyamuni mentioned *"yuzhou"* and anything else like that. But Buddhism follows the traditional usage of *"shi jie"* (世界) in ancient India, and it has the similar meaning with *"yuzhou"*. Here, the word *"shi"* refers to the time passing by (the past, the present and the future), and the word *"jie"* means orientations (the space of such ten dimensions as east, south, west, north, southeast, northeast, southwest, northwest, above and below); therefore, it has the similar meaning with *"yuzhou"*.

So, how could Sakyamuni utter such remarks as "the edge of the universe" or "edge of the world"? That is a story fabricated by Li Hongzhi. And also, he professes that the universe "has its edge", that what the Buddha knew was merely "a smaller universe", and that what he knows is the "large universe" instead; he is not only talking at random, but very madly.

Notes:
1. *Zhuan Falun*, pp. 68 & 69.
2. See *The Sutra of Metaphor of Arrows*, in the *Middle Agama Sutra*.
3. *Falun Dafa Interpretation*, p. 18.
4. Ibid, p. 29.
5. Stephen W. Hawking, a British scientist still alive, is thought to be the greatest scientist after Albert Einstein. Outstanding in the research of black

holes, he has been popular all over the world over the recent decade with his science-popularization work *A Brief History of Time.*

6. See The Explanation of Source of the Tao, *The Writings of Huainanzi.*（淮南子・原道訓）

Li Hongzhi's Flippancy and Indiscretion

The refutation and analysis above are about some relative abstruse or complicated issues. In fact, Li Hongzhi has made mistakes even in very simple questions.

Now, let's give three obvious examples.

A Mistake about "Five Kinds of Supernatural Abilities"

Li Hongzhi said,

"Buddhism promotes wu tong(五通five kinds of supernatural abilities): rouyan tong (the theurgy of physical eyes), tianyan tong (the theurgy of tianyan), huiyan tong (the theurgy of huiyan), fayan tong (the theurgy of fayan), and foyan tong (the theurgy of foyan). These are the five levels of tianmu (theurgical vision, an imaginary eye in Taoist and Buddhist practice), and each level can be subdivided into upper, middle and lower sub-levels." ①

Some Buddhist scriptures (for example, the *Abhidharmakosasastra* and the *Mahaprajnaparamita-sastra*) do record *"wu tong"* (theurgy or supernatural abilities), which refers in most cases to the reward of heretics in their meditation practice, in comparison, the cultivation achievements of bodhisattva in Buddhism are called *"liu tong"* (六通six kinds of supernatural abilities). No matter whether they are called "*wu tong*" or "*liu tong*", however, they are not "the five general levels of *tianmu*" as Li Hongzhi has mentioned.

Then, what is "*wu tong*" or "*liu tong*"? According the 18th volume of the *Abhidharmakosa-sastra*（俱舍論） as well as other scriptures such as the *Essay on the Meaning of Mahayana*（大乘義章）, the so-called "supernatural abilities" are as follows:

1. Shen Jing Zhi Zheng Tong: Also known as "*shen zu tong*" （神足通） or "*shen tong*"（身通）. A meditator who has reached a fairly high level is able to travel freely from and to various miraculous realms.

2. Tian Yan Zhi Zheng Tong: Also known as "*tian yan tong*"（天眼通）. It means the obtainment of vision belonging to the form realm (a man lives in the desire realm), that is, powerful vision surpassing that of ordinary human beings.

3. Tian Er Zhi Zheng Tong: Also known as "*tian er tong*"（天耳通）. It means the obtainment of hearing belonging to the form realm, that is, powerful hearing surpassing that of ordinary human beings.

4. Ta Xin Zhi Zheng Tong: Also known as "*ta xin tong*" （他心通）. It means the supernatural ability to read others' minds.

5. Su Ming Zhi Zheng Tong: Also known as "*su ming tong*" （宿命通）. It means the psychic power to tell the past and future of oneself and all the other living beings.

6. Lou Jin Zhi Zheng Tong: Also known as "*lou jin tong*"（漏盡通）. "*Lou*" (outflows) is another name of "defilement". It refers to the highest realm where a greatly virtuous Buddhist has extinguished all the source of his contaminations.

As it is indicated above, the so-called "*tian mu tong*" (天目通 the supernatural power of psychic vision) is merely one of the five or six kinds of supernatural abilities, how can one allege that "the supernatural vision" is divided into five levels and is named "*wu tong*"?

A Mistake about "Three Realms"

Li Hongzhi says,

> "*The 'san jie'* (三界) *in religion refers to the 9 levels of Heavens or 33 levels of Heavens, or to say, above the sky, on the ground and under the ground, they constitute all the living beings within the 'san jie'. He propagates that all the creatures in the Heavens of 33 levels have to undergo the six kinds of rebirth in samsara...Buddhism promotes to make haste to practice and cultivate Buddhism in this life. When are you not going to practice if not now?*"②

Possibly Li has learned his knowledge about "*san jie*" (Three Realms of Samsara) from Chinese folk supernatural tales now that he misunderstands it as "above the sky, on the ground and under the ground". Anyone with a little Buddhist knowledge knows that the so-called "*san jie*" absolutely does not mean "above the sky", "on the ground" or "under the ground"; instead, it refers to the desire realm, the form realm and the non-form realm, which are also known as "*san yeou*" (三有three kinds of existence). The idea of "three kinds of realms" (three kinds of existence) was closely related to the mythic tradition of Brahmanism in the ancient India, and the division of all realms and levels is related to the doctrine of transmigration (samsara) and the realm of meditation. However, the "three kinds of realms" are very complicated,③ and it is not easy to grasp their structure in a short while. The following is merely an outline of them:

The Desire Realm

The desire realm is a world inhabited by such living beings as have sexuality and appetite. It can be divided into 6 levels: Heavens (subdivided into 6 levels, inhabited by the Sons of Heavens with Six Kinds of Desires), asura, human beings (respectively living in four large continents), animals, starved ghosts and hells (subdivided into 18 levels).

The Form Realm

This realm is above the desire realm, and is a place inhabited by such living beings as have gotten rid of sexuality and appetite. This realm is still of physical existence (form), where there are physical bodies, palaces and gardens which are all wonderful and beautiful. In the light of the four realms of meditation, the form realm can be divided as many as 18 levels of Heavens (three levels of Heavens at the first level of meditation, three levels of Heavens at the second level of meditation, three levels of Heavens at the third level of meditation, and 9 levels of Heavens at the fourth level of medication).

The Non-form Realm

This realm has surpassed the form realm; it contains no physical forms at all, and all living beings exist in the form of consciousness in a very profound realm. The non-form realm can be subdivided into four levels of Heavens (the Realm of Infinite Space, the Realm of Infinite Consciousness, the Realm of Nothing Whatsoever, and the Realm of Neither Cognition Nor Non-Cognition).

The above indicates that possibly Li does not know what the "three kinds of realms" mean in Buddhism, and that his idea that the "three kinds of realms" can be divided into "above the sky, on the ground and under the ground" probably comes from folk stories or tales.

Ginger Is Not Included into "Hun" (葷)

Li Hongzhi says,

> *"The abstention from hun just came from primitive Buddhism… In fact, the hun at that time did not refer to various meat; instead, it refers to shallots, ginger, garlic and things as such… Anyone who eats such things may produce strong smells and thus affect others' meditation, seriously molesting others in practice.*

That was why such a rule was established, which viewed such things as hun, forbidding people from eating them."④

This passage should be a result of hearsay.

Actually, the primitive Buddhism merely prescribed that no garlic should be eaten. Only in the Mahayana scriptures (the *Shurangama Sutra* and the *Brahmajala Sutra*) about four hundred years later was it stipulated that "five kinds of *hun*" should not be eaten. The five kinds of *hun* are also called "*wu xin*" (五葷peppery tastes), refer to five kinds of plants with strong smells: garlic, shallot, leek, onion and *xingqu* (yielded in India, not available in China). As for other spice plants, such as ginger, capsicums, peppery, aniseeds, Chinese cinnamons and fennels, they are not included into the prohibited.

Why do Buddhist scriptures prohibit Buddhists from eating the five kinds of *hun*? The *Shurangama Sutra* lists five reasons and put them very seriously, but the major ones are three anyhow: They stimulate sexuality if they are cooked, easily provoke anger if they are not cooked, and produce strong smells no matter they are cooked or not; in the former two cases, they do harm the eaters themselves in practice, and in the latter case they disturb other practitioners.⑤

As it is shown above, Li has misunderstood this issue at three points:

1. Buddhism did not promote the taboo against "*hun*" in the stage of primitive Buddhism; instead, such prohibition did not emerge until in the Mahayana scriptures four hundred years later after the Buddha's passing.
2. Ginger（薑） is not included in the five kinds of taboo food.
3. The very reason why Buddhism prohibits the eating of those five kinds of *hun* is mainly because of three reasons: They may stir up sexuality, stimulate anger and produce smells disturbing other people. Li Hongzhi knows only one of them.

The above three points are trivial knowledge, and possibly any common Buddhists are familiar with them, but Li makes mistakes even about so simple knowledge, that indicates how few books he has read.

Notes:

1. *Zhuan Falun*, p. 58.
2. Ibid, p. 88.
3. As for detail, see the author's *Selection of Buddhist Doctrines*, Chapter 4, Section 4, Three Realms and Six Levels, and the Transmigration of Life and Death (三界六道生死輪迴). And also, readers can consult *A Detailed of the Three Realms system Spoken by Buddha*, by a monastic Hongren (釋宏忍: 佛說三界天體系詳細表). Published by Taipei Lao Ku Culture Foundation Inc.
4. *Zhuan Falun*, p. 306; *Falun Dafa Interpretation*, p. 96.
5. See Rev. Shengyan, *Inquiries into the Dharma* (釋聖嚴: 學佛群疑), p. 16. Taipei Dongchu Publishing Company, 1996, revised edition. The author's *Fundamentals of Precept Studies*, pp. 315 & 327.

Is Li Hongzhi Writing Supernatural Stories?

In Li's "works", there are not only a lot of plagiarized terms from Buddhism, Taoism and modern science, but also some ancient spirits and fairies, and even some supernatural experiences of his own. They seem like some folk supernatural tales, and are very interesting in a certain sense.

Snake Spirits

Let's appreciate a story about a snake spirit at first, and Li says it is his own experience.

"When I went to Guizhou to propagate the Gong for the first time, somebody came to me when I was giving the class, saying his master's master wanted to see me, and his master's master was who and who, and that he had practiced for many many years. At the first glance I had noticed that man had negative aura around him, which was very vicious. And he had an ill yellow face. I said I would not like to see him, for I had no time. In that way I declined. Consequently that old man was annoyed, and began to make troubles with me, disturbing me every day. I am a man who is not willing to have quarrels with people, and moreover, I have not enough reason to fight against

them. I just clear up the bad things he brought; having cleared them up, I continued to propagate my dharma.

"In the Ming Dynasty (明朝) *, there was a man who practiced the Tao. As he practiced the Tao, his body was possessed by a snake. Afterwards, the man died before he made his final achievement of practice, and the snake incarnated itself in the form of that man since it had possessed his body. That visitor's master's master was just that snake who incarnated itself in man through practice. It did not change its nature, so it showed its previous form to disturb me. I thought it too outrageous, so I grasped it in my hand, using a very powerful kind of gong (a kind of supernatural force obtained through practice and cultivation), which is called hua gong* (化功) *. I thus dissolved the hind part of its body. After its hind body turned into liquid, the rest part above its waist fled back.*

"One day, the director of our instruction center in Guizhou (貴 州) *was sent for by its disciple's disciple, who said his Grand-Master wanted to see her. The director thus went. She saw nothing but a dim figure sitting there in the dark after she entered a cave. The eyes of the figure glazed in green. When it opened its eyes, the cave was lighted, but when it closed its eyes, the cave became dark again. He talked in local dialect, 'Li Hongzhi is going to come here again. This time none of us is going to do that once more; I was wrong, I did not know Li has come to rescue people.' The disciple's disciple asked him, 'The Grand- Master, will you stand up, please? What is the matter with your legs?' He replied, 'I can't. My legs are hurt.' When he was asked how they got hurt, he began to describe how he disturbed me. At the Oriental Health Exposition in 1993 in Beijing, once again he disturbed me. Because he always committed wrongdoings, hindering me from propagating Dafa, I destroyed him completely. After he was annihilated, his senior and junior fellow apprentices wanted to revenge him, but I said something at that time, and they were shocked. Since they were*

so frightened, no one dare revenge him anymore, and they come to know what a matter it is." ①

It is such a tall story that it is even more bizarre than *The Legend of the White Snake* (白蛇傳)! Now, the author tries to paraphrase it, which might arouse the readers' more interest in it:

The story says that as early as in the Ming Dynasty, there was a snake which practiced and achieved the form of man, it surprisingly survived until today, and turned out to become a rare old snake spirit. More than 400 years later, just because the Great Master Li Hongzhi was reluctant to do it a favor by condescending to pay it a visit, the snake demon felt that it had lost its face, so it constantly disturbed Li, deliberately interfering Li's propagating the cosmic law. Master Li is a man of great compassion, so he did not care at first. But that animal did not appreciate what was good for it, continuing to disturb Li. So Master Li had to take a severe method, dissolving its hind body into water. Strangely enough, this snake did not die although it had lost half its body, just like a gecko; it fled back although it had only half of its body left. Li was not the only one who knew this event, he had two witnesses! The director of the instruction center in Guiyang and that demon 's disciple's disciple once paid a visit to the snake demon, and the latter regretted its offence against Master Li. Unexpectedly, however, that demon could not change its nature, and it dare to come to Beijing to interfere Li in 1993. So, Master Li was forced to annihilate it, eliminating it both physically and spiritually. Its fellow apprentices wanted to revenge it against Li, but they were deterred by Li's a few words. Up to now, those several trivial demons finally understood that this Master Li was the number-one "great sage of the whole universe" incarnated in the form of man in these billions of years, and was billions of billions more powerful than the Monkey King Sun Wukong (孫悟空), who was merely a "Great Sage Equal to Heaven"! No one wanted to revenge the dead snake anymore, of course.

So, it seems that Li is much more powerful than Fahai (法海)! That Fahai could only encage the poor snake demon Madame White Snake below the Leifeng Stupa (雷峰塔), but Li was able to dissolve the hind body of the snake demon into water at his first stroke, and annihilate it completely at the second.

Demonic Possession

Li Hongzhi seems to be especially fond of the term "possession" （附體）, and he often tells such stories of their kinds. Then, what is "possession"? According to him, all the practitioners who have practiced in improper ways, for example, those professed *qigong* masters, have had their bodies possessed by snake demons, fox demons, weasel demons and so forth. Having possessed the bodies of practitioners, these spirits or demons are able to receive the benefits of practice and cultivation; in other words, a man's practice consummates that of those animals, and gradually they will become powerful demons, and even incarnate themselves into the form of man. But those who possess the bodies of others are certainly devils, and the principle of the universe does not allow an animal to consummate its practice, hence they would be annihilated at certain moment.

The above is a generalization of Li's main points; now let's quote a passage from his original text as proof:

"Some people say that animals can practice, say that foxes can practice, and say that a certain snake can practice, and so forth. Actually, it is not that they can practice. At the first stage, they know nothing about practice; it is their inborn instinct. Under certain conditions, in some certain environments, such instinct can play its role after long, and such animals can achieve gong, and will be able to display some power gained through the practice and cultivation of gong. Where such case happens, it will become able, or it will have supernatural ability if in our term in the past...It does not have the nature of human beings, so it cannot practice as a man does. Without man's qualities, it certainly turns into devils after it finishes its practice and cultivation, so it is not allowed to practice. That is why it is predestined to be annihilated. And it knows it, too."

In this passage, Li alleges that animals (such as snakes, foxes and so on) have the instinct to practice, but they are predestined to become devils after they finish their practice and thus be killed. After that, he continues with that all those professed *qigong* masters have had their bodies possessed by such animals, and that their *qigong* is nothing but witchcraft.

> *"How many people among the qigong practitioners all over the country have had their bodies possessed? If I speak out that number, I am afraid many people dare not practice anymore, for that number is rather shocking! Especially, those professed qigong masters all have had their bodies possessed, and what they propagate are nothing but such things."*②

Such animals are not only able to possess a man's body to practice, but also control his brains, and even kill his original spirit. In this way, they will finally possess the whole body of that man. So, Master Li continues,

> *"As a matter of fact, he did not develop his tian mu (psychic eyes), it is that animal that has controlled his brains, that animal sees with its eyes, transmitting information to his brains, so he thought he had developed his tian mu. When he exercises his power of gong, that animal will extend its small paws from the side of his body; once he exercises his power of gong, that small animal will extend its tongue, licking the focus, the swelling part of his body. People like this are in a large number, their possession is caused by themselves."*③

> *"This phenomenon is especially obvious and especially common among today's practitioners; while possessing the bodies of practitioners, they even kill the original spirits of people, get into niwangong (dantian), squatting there. He looks to be a human being, but in fact he is not. Such cases have occurred and are very common now."*④

Animal possession is so dreadful, and Master Li has annihilated the old snake demon so completely, so he has done a greatly charitable deed. But here arises a big problem: a snake which has lived four hundred years and now incarnated itself in the form of man should have been viewed as a global treasure, let alone a national one, and the UN will certainly include it into the list of "cultural heritage" which most deserves protection in the world. But now, it was annihilated by Master Li, what can he do if the animal protection groups of all countries arise to protest in succession? And what can he do if the UN asks him to take his responsibility?

Original Spirit

Taoism has three frequent words "*jing*" (精the material foundation of vitality), *qi*（氣） and *shen* (神soul), and these three are also known as "*san yuan*" (the three of the original), namely, original *jing*（元精）, original *qi* （元氣）and original spirit（元神）. Original *jing* usually refers to the semen of a male, original *qi* refers to the vitality of a person's physical body, and the original spirit refers to the soul of a man, the dominator of life. A Taoist knack in practice stresses to "refine semen into *qi*, refine *qi* into soul, and refine soul for the return to voidness"（煉精化氣，煉氣化神，煉神還虛）. Once a practitioner elevates himself up to the realm of the "integration of the three of the original"（三元合一）, he will have consummated himself in Taoist practice.⑤

Surprisingly, Li Hongzhi divides the "original spirit" as a major spirit and secondary spirits, and what is more, one person can have several such secondary spirits. That is really wonderful. It must be of Li's originality now that we cannot find any similar idea of others. Now, let's have a look at how Li himself explains it:

> *"Now, I come to another question. A person has his secondary original spirit (secondary consciousness) in addition to his major original spirit (major consciousness). Some people have one, two, three, four or even five secondary spirits. Such secondary original spirits do not necessarily have the same sex as the right person, some may be male, and some may be female; they are all*

different. Actually, the major original spirit does not necessarily have same sex as the physical body does, either, for we have discovered many males now have female original spirits, and vice versa. That exactly complies with the natural phenomenon as Taoism has described, that is, yin and yang oppose each other, and yin prospers while yang declines.

"Secondary original spirits are often at higher levels than major ones; especially, some people's secondary original spirits are especially advanced. Secondary original spirits are different from possession; they are born together with you from the same womb, have the same name as you do, and they are a part of your body. In daily life, people's thinking and doing are dominated by major original spirits. Secondary original spirits mainly play a role in preventing major original spirits from committing wrongdoings, but secondary original spirits can do nothing when major original spirits are very obdurate. Secondary original spirits cannot be deluded by the society of mediocre people, but major original spirits are often enticed.

"Some secondary original spirits are at such high levels that they may have achieved consummation if they have made a little more efforts. Secondary original spirits wish to practice, but they can do nothing if major ones do not. One day when a major original spirit enjoys its climax in qigong practice, it suddenly has the impulse to learn Gong, to elevate itself through practice and cultivation; its motive is simple, of course, and is not mixed with the pursuit of fame and interests. Secondary original spirits feel very happy: I wish to practice, but I have no say in that matter; now that you want to practice, that is just what I have desired. But where to find a master? The secondary original spirit is very capable, and it leaves the physical body to see a greatly enlightened person that it knew in its previous life. Some secondary original spirits are at very high levels, so they depart from the physical bodies which they depend upon. After its arrival, it tells that enlightened person that it wants to

borrow the latter's Gong. That person knows it is a good man, and thinks it his responsibility to help the latter to practice. In this way, the secondary original spirit successfully borrows the Gong."⑥

What structure does the ego of us as human beings have on earth? Confucianism has the dichotomy of the "nature as Heavenly Principles" (天理之性) and the "attributes of physical bodies" (氣質之性). Buddhism has the doctrine that "one mind can be divided as two gates" (一心開二門), and in western psychology, there are the concepts such as "actual self", "self" and the "self in subconsciousness". So, it is all right that Li divides the "original spirit" into two (major original spirit and secondary original spirits). But the problem is that he does not explain why there may be several secondary original spirits. Strangely, only physical bodies of human beings can have the difference of male and female, but original spirits are not physical bodies, how can they be divided as males and females? His idea at this point is obviously unreasonable. What is more unacceptable is that "secondary original spirits" can leave the physical body they rely on to visit a master and borrow Gong! This is a fiction about the supernatural, but not any propaganda of "Dafa".

Overall, the above mentioned writings do impress readers with a fiction about the supernatural. Li Hongzhi is not writing supernatural stories, of course; only that he mixes such plots into his "cosmic law", impressing people with such disparity, and thus affecting the credibility of his "cosmic law".

Notes:
1. *Zhuan Falun*, pp. 233-234.
2. Ibid, pp. 130-132.
3. Ibid, p. 135.
4. Ibid, 137.
5. As for the cultivation of the three of the original, see Volume Yuan titled "The Synthetism of the

Three Schools of Confucianism, Buddhism and Taoism" and other sections in *A Genuine Taoist Guide to Cultivation of Nature and Life.*
6. *Zhuan Falun*, pp. 126-128.

The Magic Use of Nouns

After the above respective refutation and analysis in all sections, we can make a summary now.

In magic shows that people usually watch, a magician can seize a pigeon out of his hat, a young girl in a wooden box can remain unhurt even if the box is penetrated with a sword or chopped with a knife, and a white paper can be suddenly turned into a bank note... Such tricks often attract audiences, especially children, who believe they are true. The key point of magic is that its "essence" is absolutely false, but it impresses people as if it is true. That is where the strength of magic shows rests in.

Li Hongzhi's "Dafa" is absolutely false, and all is his own fiction, but "Falun Gong" has attracted some people all over the world, and some people even believe in it without a shadow of doubt. Why is that? In addition to political reasons, there are two other major elements: first, just as we have analyzed in Section Two, if one is able to exercise with the five sets of actions every day, his physical conditions will certainly be improved within about three months. That is not because of any "Dafa"; instead, it is completely the result of the stretching movement and meditation sitting. Second, Li is good at mixing together some Buddhist terms, Taoist terms, tales of ghosts and spirits, and frequent nouns in newspapers and journals. It can easily play a "magic role" to those who have poor knowledge or mediocre analytic ability.

Overall, the nouns that Li has used can be largely divided into four types:

1. Buddhist Terms

For example, "Fofa", "Falun", "*yeli*" (effective of karma), "*san jie*" (three realms), "*mofa*" (the latter dharma), "*zheng fa*" (true dharma), "Buddhahood", "reality-bodies", "arhat", "bodhisattva", "enlightenment", "send to the heaven", "emptiness" (sunya), "*xiumi*" (to practice the esoteric), "*jiachi*" (to aid and bless), "consecration", "*guanding*" (sprinkling water on the head", "non-duality dharma-gate", "Sakyamuni", "Mahavairocana", "*sanqian daqian shi jie*" (One Billion Worlds), and so forth.

2. Taoist Terms

For example, "*zhoutian*" (a whole round, a whole course), "*caiqi*" (to absorb *qi*), "*dantian*", "*xuanguan*" (the mysterious gate to the Taoism), "Five Elements", "original spirit", "secondary original spirits", "*san hua ju ding*" (The quintessence of the three of *jing*, *qi* and spirit converge at the top of the head), and so on.

3. Common Nouns about Supernatural Things

For example, "possession", "*tianmu*" (supernatural vision), "*liti*" (departure from physical body), "*se mo*" (devils in physical forms), "*yin qi*" (evil aura), "fox", "snake", "weasel", and the like.

4. Nouns of Natural Science

For example, "universe", "molecule", "atom", "electron", "quark", "neutrino", "field", "celestial body", "matter", "space", "galaxy", "energy" and "material", etc.

The "Fa" that Li Hongzhi propagandizes is essentially a muddle of the above-mentioned nouns, which he has taken in a common sense or literally. His theory is largely as such:

- The "Gong" that Li Hongzhi has propagated is something at the highest level in the multi-level universe. The Buddhism that Sakyamuni promoted 2,500 years ago was at a low level. The Tao that Laotze propagated in China more than 2,000 years ago was a thing within the boundary of our Galaxy. But Falun Gong teaches people to practice in the light of the principle of evolution of the universe, the highest quality of the universe. Practicing so great a thing equates to practicing the universe. So, his "Dafa" surpasses both Buddhism and Taoism.

- Buddhism has begun to decline since the passing of Sakyamuni. After it was introduced into China, some traditional things have been mixed into Buddhism; especially, the Chan School has clung to prejudice and extremely wrong knowledge. As for the practice and cultivation of Taoism, a master imparts his things to disciples secretly, and it is not open to the society. At present, Li Hongzhi is the only one who publicly propagates the highest "Dafa" in the universe. This sufficiently shows the greatest compassion to the people in this world, and it has been unprecedented for thousands of millions of years. So, Li need not feel ashamed although he easily views himself as a "master".

- All those who favor "Falun Dafa" are Li's "disciples". As the result of practice of "Falun Dafa", one's spirit (soul) will be reborn in the space at a higher level in the universe even if his physical body dies. Or otherwise, those who do not believe in nor practice "Falun Gong" will vanish both physically and spiritually after their death. In the universe, there is nothing more dreadful than the "annihilation both of physical body and spirit".

- Li's "*fashen*" (reality-bodies) will embed a "Falun" in a person's *dantian* (lower belly) once he listens to Li's lecture or read his works on "Fa". This "Falun" is a miniature of the universe; it can provide enormous energy for a practitioner, help his "*gong*" grow, and form a piece of spiral "pole of *gong*" (功柱) on the top of his head. The higher his pole of *gong* is, the higher level he is at. After the pole of *gong* grows up to a certain height, the practitioner's "original spirit" and "secondary original spirit" can even depart from his physical body to do things alone; his eyes will be able to "develop supernatural vision", seeing a real world that an ordinary man cannot.

- Now that Li Hongzhi is propagating such great "*gongfa*", it is natural that he is envied and set up by "devils". And the believers of such "*gongfa*" will certainly be disturbed by various "devils". This is a test for the practitioners, and they need not be frightened. Anyone who opposes "Falun Dafa" is a "devil"; if you pass such test, your "*gong*" will grow faster.

The above is the outline of Li's theory about his "Dafa". In order to express such theory, he abuses many nouns in the afore-mentioned four types. In fact, some of those nouns have very profound meanings, which he has no possibility to understand due to his poor knowledge and his extreme self-righteousness; as for Buddhist terms "emptiness", "reality-bodies", "karma", "non-duality dharma-gate", "dependent origination" and so on, for example, he has misunderstood them all. For another example, such concepts as "time and space", "neutrino", "wave" and "field" in natural science have be based on precise tests with sophisticated instruments and profound mathematic demonstration; without experimental facility or mathematic knowledge, it is impossible to understand such concepts, and one can only parrot them by taking them literally.

What is more, Li likes to coin new words in order to show he is different; actually he has the motive of a "magician" when he does so. He shamelessly brags as follows:

"I do not like the superficial grammar or words of modern language which have been standardized all along, so I often do not use standard grammar or words when I propagate my dharma...

*"How can the dharma of the universe be standardized by the culture of human beings? So long it can make clear the principles of dharma, I would like to make the culture of mankind in an open state, get rid of those standards and restraints, and use them freely; in order to express Dafa clearly, I would use them as I wish...As for the choice of words, I basically use them as I wish, for example, I often write "cheng du" (程度) as "cheng du" (成度). I think that the word "cheng" (成) should be used to indicate how much a thing has been completed. I like to write "zhen xiang" (真相) as "zhen xiang" (真象), for I think that the actual appearance should be described with this "xiang" (象). I love to write "jue" (绝) as "jue" (决) because I think this latter word has more weight. I have chosen to replace "hong" (弘) with "hong" (洪), for the word "hong" (洪) is more suitable for the cosmic law, and so on and on."*①

All common words in daily use have their fair fixed meanings, such meanings have been established through common practice after long, and people can communicate only by these words. Furthermore, people think by means of language, so the meanings of language work on the rational thinking of people; once the meanings of languages are ambiguous, the thinking will thus fall into disorder. This anyone is able to understand who has a little knowledge about the function of language. Li Hongzhi deliberately breaches the existing rules of language, he simply intends to confuse others and render some muddled people to believe in him.

Concretely, he deliberately makes use of a muddle of common terms in Buddhism, making people take them literally and thus convincing them that what he propagandizes is the true dharma of Buddhism. But once you further research what he says, you have such doubts as "how Buddhism can be like this". Then, he will firmly tell you that what he says is not the Buddhism of Sakyamuni, that is, not the Buddhism in your previous conception, rather, it is the "cosmic law" surpassing all anything else. Usually, many people know little about the terms of Buddhism, Taoism and science;

having been deceived as such, they dare have no doubts anymore. Once a few people of insight who have cool heads are not muddled by him and dare question and criticize him, he will castigate them as "ruffians of science", "ruffians of culture", "ruffians of *qigong*", "evil force", "ruffians of religion" and so forth.② Scholars are reluctant to meddle in others' affairs. Once they are cursed as such, they probably dare not ask for such troubles anymore. That is the "magic use", and Li Hongzhi is actually spiritually fooling others.

It is acceptable to use existing words to express new conceptions and even coin some new ones once the existing words are thought insufficient to express some abstruse thoughts. Such cases are common in the works of some Western philosophers such as Immanuel Kant and Martin Heidegger (1889—1976). Li Hongzhi, who has a mere middle school degree, has no profound thought at all; he is even unable to use words correctly, and the <Hong Yin> that he has written is unreasonable at all, but he boasts that the case is that he is "not restrained by the regulations of grammar and words of mankind". It is arrogant enough to make a horse laugh.

For example, he substitutes "*hong chuan*" (洪傳) (literally means to "be propagated by Li Hongzhi) for "*hong chuan*" (弘傳) (to propagate), simply adding his name to the expression. It is extremely childish and jejune. As modern psychology has proved, a person's arrogance in words and behaviors are proportionate to his inferiority complex. In addition to the motive of "magic use", Li's abuses and invention of terms should also be a result of subconsciousness to cover up his superficiality.

What is worse is the problem of "self-deception". When he employs a lot of such terms for "magic use", perhaps he himself was clear that it was false at first, and he did so on purpose to make others believe in his "Dafa". But after long, the lies he told gradually play a role of "self-suggestion" in his own mind, he himself becomes convinced of them; now that he himself has been convinced of them, he certainly cannot allow others to have any doubt. This is called the effect of "negative self psychological suggestion" in modern Western psychology.

As for such an effect, the Consciousness-only Theory in Buddhism can help us to have a better understanding. Our consciousness at the 8th level (alaya consciousness) contains numberless "seeds", and these "seeds" will embody themselves as concrete behaviors in certain circumstances; meanwhile, any concrete behaviors will turn into new "seeds" in turn. So, the repetition of same actions or words can form powerful "new seeds" in one's own consciousness at the 8th level. These "new seeds" consequentially dominate the person's consciousness and behaviors in all aspects. That is the principle of "negative self psychological suggestion", and also the best commentary on the popular saying that "man is the slave of habits". Has Li Hongzhi been trapped in such effects already? He should have deep self-reflection himself.

Notes:
1. *Essentials for Further Advances* (Vol. Two), pp. 30 & 31.
2. *Essentials for Further Advances*, pp. 135 & 148.

Falun Gong and Politics

It has been 18 years from May 1992 when Li Hongzhi began to teach people to practice Falun Gong in Changchun, Northeast China up to the present (October 2010). In these 18 years, it seems that Falun Gong has had an indispensable bond with politics; whatever it is good or bad, it is a bond anyhow. Falun Gong has been closely related to politics in terms of its origination, the social environment when it was founded, its sudden world reputation and so on. In recent years, it seems that Falun Gong itself has dissimilated, leaving people with the impression of a "pure political body". It is seldom seen in the history of world religion that a religious body degenerates into a political one. If our impression as such is not wrong, then what result will Falun Gong come up with after it turns into a political group? This is the main point of this section.

The Emergence of Falun Gong

The emergence of Falun Gong certainly was closely related to Li Hongzhi's personal background, of course. According to the publications under his control, Li used to work at the song and dance ensemble of the Forest Squadron of Armed Police Troops of Jilin Province at first and then at the Changchun City Cereals Company before he began to teach Falun Gong.① The song and dance ensemble was a unit which took art show as its profession, and its staff members had a large circle of acquaintances and were good at drawing the attention of the mass. Before the reform and opening of the mainland to the outside world in 1978, so to speak, those who were able to have a job at cereals units in a big city were "chosen few";② with sufficient ration of food and clothing as well as s cushy job, Li was thus able to pay visits to Buddhist and Taoist monastics in his leisure time. Concretely, Li's background was closely related to the political situation in the mainland at that time; if he had not had such a good job, his subsistence would become a big problem, how could he think about his "cosmic law"? And if he had not worked for a unit of art shows, possibly he would not know how to draw the multitude to listen to his "Fa".

The years from 1988 to 1992 witnessed the formation and establishment of Falun Gong; it was a period when the political atmosphere in the mainland was weird and gloomy, and the people over there felt perplexed and swayed in their mind. But strangely enough, Taiwan was also in fierce turbulence in these four years;③ even the world situation was at an unparalleled moment—The social system in the East European countries changed, and the Soviet Union suddenly collapsed. All these happened in those four years. Were these coincidental or destined? One cannot but suspect that the ancient Chinese people's philosophy of history about "*yuan, huei, yuen* and *shi*" （元、會、運、世） is somewhat reasonable.④

In those four years, the "June 4 Incident" happened in the mainland in 1989, which Deng Xiaoping called a "right-wing riot". At that time, the reform and opening to the outside world has been performed for ten years, it had caused many side effects despite its remarkable economic achievements; for example, money worship had caused the moral degeneration in the society, and beneficiaries in the reform and opening worried about the instability of policies, and the narrow-minded feared that the socialist system in the mainland would be abandoned. All such thoughts had formed hidden torrents in the society, and would probably converge into a crisis in reality. This situation did not change until Deng delivered his "A Speech in the Southwards Trip" in 1992. In these four years, therefore, it was inevitable that people felt disquieted. Whenever they feel disquieted, people would look for spiritual guarantee, and easily accept strange things.

Overall, it was in such a social and political situation that Li Hongzhi established his Falun Gong, and it was not that he himself was capable enough to manage it alone, let alone that the "history of the cosmic law" has predestined him to do so as he has professed. Li Hongzhi happened to learn *qigong* in 1988 and touched some common knowledge of Buddhism and Taoism in such atmospheres. Also in such a situation of political ambiguity and people's disquiet, Li propagated the "Dafa" that he has made up, unexpected received support from many people.

The Development of Falun Gong

Li Hongzhi seemed to have been lucky all the time in the decade after Falun Gong was established. According to the CPC's official information,⑤ Li Hongzhi founded the Falun Dafa Research Society in Beijing and held the position of director immediately after he made up Falun Gong in Changchun in 1992. Soon afterwards, 39 general Falun Gong instruction stations were set up in succession in provinces, autonomous regions and municipal cities directly under the Central Government; under these general instruction stations there were more than 1,900 instruction stations, and under these instruction stations were more than 28,000 exercise sites.

One can imagine Falun Gong's prosperity from the point of the numbers of its organizational units; such prosperity was a result of the social environment in the mainland at that time, but not really an achievement of Li's "cosmic law". However, Li Hongzhi did have some "magic power", and such "power" rests in that he made up a set of "Gong" which happened to meet the requirement of people's disquiet at that time. Generally, people would commonly use the word "magic" or "supernatural" to describe such cases in which one achieves something an ordinary man cannot or one has such good luck that it is seldom seen.

Falun Gong performed many large-scaled activities in the mainland in the 7 years from its establishment to April 25, 1999. Those activities were mostly masterminded and directed by the

Falun Dafa Research Society and the general instruction stations in all places. Those activities were under the banner of "spread of Fa", "exchange of practice experiences from different exercise sites", "celebration" or "commemoration" and so on. That certainly caused the authorities' misgivings; the CPC, which had been good at organization and depended up the "mass line" to spring up, was inevitably very sensitive to those large-scaled mass activities. But how to stop them? It could hardly find an excuse to directly ban such kinds of activities which easily assembled thousands of people to practice Falun Gong in the name of doing good deeds. The only thing it could do was to release some articles in newspapers and journals to criticize Li Hongzhi, and confiscate booklets and audio and video products sold among people with the excuse that they are illegal publications without permission. Such a trivial measure was just what Li Hongzhi hoped for: It simply gave him an excuse to launch the masses to protest against the authorities in charge. And more importantly, the confiscation of his books turned out to be a kind of sales promotion. There was a saying among ancients, which said that "There are three happy things for intellectuals: the wedding night, the passing of an imperial examination, and the reading of banned books stealthily at night". Banned books spread and sold among the multitude can hardly be really banned; the more you ban them, the more they become popular; Lee Mao (李某) in Taiwan was just the best example of this kind: his reputation was mostly based on the confiscation and prohibition of his books at that time, the more the authorities banned his books, the more they were sold. In this way, Lee Mao obtained both his fame and economic profits. Falun Gong paraded itself with its teaching free of charge, but incomes are needed for individuals' subsistence and organizational activities, and Li Hongzhi's major incomes probably come from the sales of his books and audio and video tapes.

The fight was rewarded. In this way, Falun Gong developed in those constant activities. Wang Zhaoguo (王兆國), who took the post of director of the United Front Department of the CPC Central Committee at that time, clearly pointed out,

*"Falun Gong wields harmful influence all over the country, and people who were deluded workers, peasants, retired cadres, intellectuals, CPC party members, democrats, independents and members of the Federation of Industry & Commerce and all other related people."*⑥

Li Hongzhi and his family became the most direct beneficiaries. Li Hongzhi immigrated as an "outstanding talent" to the USA in 1996, two years later, his wife and child settled in New York. Li Hongzhi, who stayed in America, claimed that he taught "only Fa instead Gong", i.e. he sent instructions, articles by telephone, fax, internet and others modern communications to the organizations at levels in the Chinese mainland, remotely controlling his believers' activities. That was how the "April 25 Incident" was brewed.

The April 25 Incident

Li Hongzhi mobilized as many as ten thousand people to besiege Zhongnanhai, the office site of the Party Central Committee on April 25, 1999. According to the official reports of the CPC, the immediate cause of this incident was mainly as follows:

On April 19, the *Science Review for Juveniles*, a school magazine of the Tianjin Normal University (天津師範大學), published an essay titled I Do Not Agree with Juveniles' Practice of *Qigong*, which was written by He Zuoxiu (何祚庥), an academician of the Chinese Academy of Sciences. This essay caused discontent among some Falun Gong believers in Tianjin, and they sat in at the school to protest. Up to 22nd, the number of protestors increased more than 3,000.

Just at that moment, Li Hongzhi suddenly arrived in Beijing at 5: 35 pm on 22nd by the flight NW087 of Northwest Airlines of the USA, with the identity of "businessman". On the following day of Li Hongzhi's entry, i.e. April 23, the protest in Tianjin Normal University quickly expanded, the number of participants zoomed to more than 6,300. In the morning of the 24th, before Li Hongzhi left China,⑦ Falun Gong exercise sites in Beijing and many other places were noticed of mobilizing "disciples" to "practice collectively" around

Zhongnanhai the next day. On April 25, more than 10,000 Falun Gong practitioners gathered on the roads around Zhongnanhai, forming a besieging situation; they protested in silence to the Party Central Committee in the way of "practice". That was an event that had never happened since the CPC's regime was established, and it turned out to be a shock wave all over the world immediately after the report by overseas media.

Possibly the CPC authorities did not know how to handle such an unprecedented affair at first. Not until three months later on July 22 did they launch an all-round counterattack, nine important departments, including the CPC Central Committee, the Ministry of Civil Affairs, the Ministry of Public Security, the United Front Work Department, the Organization Department of the CPC Central Committee, the Publicity Department of the CPC Central Committee, the Ministry of Human Resources and Social Security, the General Administration of Press and Publication, and the Central Committee of the Communist Youth League, dispatched notices, decisions, announces, speeches and other files in succession. They all defined the "nature" of Li Hongzhi and his "Dafa", and severely told their subordinates what to do and what not to do. And then, secondary departments, media and so on were mobilized to encircle and suppress "Falun Gong": the *People's Daily* published seven commentary articles in succession, the Xinhua News Agency, the *Guangming Daily*, the *Qiushi Magazine* and other official media followed up one by one. In this way, Li Hongzhi suddenly became a world famous man.

The "Definition of the Nature" by All Departments of the Authorities

It is very necessary to review the "definition of the nature" of Li Hongzhi and his organization made by the departments at that time, and it will be useful in predicting the future. Some representative examples are as follows⑧:

The Notice about the Prohibition of CPC Party Members' Practicing "Falun Dafa" issued by the CPC Central Committee said,

"It is a serious political struggle to disclose and criticize Li Hongzhi and his 'Falun Dafa'. Party organizations at all levels should fully realize the 'complexity and arduousness' of this struggle."

Wang Zhaoguo, director of the United Front Work Department of the CPC Central Committee said in his "Circular Notice to All Democratic Parties, Federation of Industry and Commerce and Independent Personages",

"The Falun Gong incident is the most serious political event after the 'June 4' political storm in 1989. The arising and spreading of 'Falun Gong' is a political struggle in which the hostile forces both at home and abroad contest for the masses and the position with our party."

The Ministry of Civil Affairs said in its <Decision about Banning the Falun Dafa Research Society>,

"As investigation proves, the Falun Dafa Research Society has not been registered by law, and it engages itself in illegal activities, propagates superstition and heresies, deludes the masses, provokes disputes, and undermines social stability. Hereby, in the light of pertinent provisions of the Rules of Registration and Administration of Social Groups, the Falun Dafa Research Society and the Falun Gong organizations that it manipulates are identified as illegal organizations and thus banned."

An editorial article in the *People's Daily* on July 22, 1999 said,

"By means of his 'Falun Gong' organizations, Li Hongzhi has promoted the 'Falun Dafa" that he has fabricated, delude the people and fool the multitude to the utmost. He has not only spiritually manipulated practitioners...but also

organizationally controlled them, done his utmost to develop national organizations, contested for the mass, and even infiltrated into some of our party and governmental institutions and important departments, attempting to develop them into political force that opposes our party and government."

The above definitions made by the institutions of the CPC indicate how serious this event had become in the mind of the CPC. Therefore, it naturally arouses considerable doubt: Is such a serious political response what Li Hongzhi likes to see or not? The answer is very important. If it belongs to the former, it will prove that Li's "spread of Fa" in the mainland in the past 8 years was false, and was merely artifice, and that his true purpose rested in politics. Furthermore, Li published two essays overseas after the "April 25 Incident", which repeatedly stressed that

"You can imagine it: there are more than one hundred million 'Falun Gong' practitioners, but only ten thousand went there. How can it be said to be a large number?"

"I wonder how long they would endure under such unfair treatment. And that is what I am worried about."

"All the people in the country have their deep understanding of Falun Gong, and the consequence thus caused will lead the people to lose their trust towards the government and leaders, and become disappointed at the Chinese government." ⑨

These remarks are actually defiance and threat against a power, and they could only worsen the antagonism and opposition between two sides. That indicate Li should be pleased at such a situation.

The Transformation into a Political Organization

After the "April 25 Incident", Li Hongzhi and his organization could not continue their activities in the mainland anymore, but they became active overseas; the period largely from 2001 to 2005 witnessed the peak of their activities overseas. In those years, people under the banner of "Falun Dafa" were often seen around the world, and they engaged with the organizations of Taiwan Independence and Tibetan Independence to protest against the CPC.

So to speak, Falun Gong is most active in Taiwan. Chen Shuibian began to reign in 2000 and was inclined to the route of "Taiwan Independence"; the supporters of Falun Gong may not agree with "Taiwan Independence", but they were in the same camp in opposing "China". It does not matter whether this "China" was the "China" as a country or the CPC, larger crowds were helpful to the scene of clamor anyhow. Therefore, reports on Falun Gong activities in the island were often seen in the newspapers and journals in Taiwan in those years. After 2004, however, Chen Shuibian' continual misdeeds had greatly provoked the Taiwan society; as a result, millions of people easily gathered in the streets to protest the unfair general election which involved the shooting case or Chen's corruption, and almost nobody paid attention to the political activities of Falun Gong anymore. From 2008 on, Ma Ying-jeou has come into power, trying hard to stabilize the peace across the Taiwan Straits, and Falun Gong's political activities attract less attention than before.

Their "practice" was in the same situation. Around 2002, Falun Gong practitioners were often seen in many parks in Taiwan and Hong Kong in the morning; they always put up such slogans as "Falun Dafa Is Good" and "Truthfulness, Compassion and Forbearance" written in red on yellow cloth banners, which were very striking. On the ground, there would be piles of promotional materials for free, and passers-by were allowed to take home as they wished. Those were just their "exercise sites"; although the numbers of practitioners at each exercise site were few, there were exercise sites in all parks. In recent years, however, such exercise sites have been seldom seen in all the parks in Taiwan and Hong Kong.

Possibly for this reason, Falun Gong has gradually turned into a purely political organization in these years. Such change can be easily seen through their conditions in Taiwan, for Taiwan is a typical place of Falun Gong activities. The most remarkable signs are as follows: a free-of-charge propaganda *Epoch Times Weekly* (大世纪周報) under the control of the Falun Dafa Research Society, Li Hongzhi's agency in Taiwan, was restructured to be the *Epoch Times* (大世纪時報) about five years ago (in the early 2005), and another weekly named the *New Epoch* (新世纪) began to be published three years ago. The newspaper and the journal are sold publicly, and are not free-of-charge pure propaganda; though their content was comprehensive, they have an obvious political orientation, that is, to disclose and criticize the CPC.

The *Epoch Times* delivered a series of editorials titled *"Nine Commentaries on the Communist Party"* (九評共產党) immediately it turned into a daily newspaper; later on, these 9 pieces of articles were compiled into a booklet in simplified Chinese, distributed for long among the tourists from the mainland to Hong Kong and Taiwan. Among the 9 articles, in fact, except for the fifth one which inveighed against Jiang Zemin (江澤民) and was a little different, all the rest lack in new content—they were mostly the copy of Kuomintang's criticism against the CPC in the serious confrontation across the Taiwan Straits in the past. However, it is just these articles that leave people with a strong impression that Falun Gong has now turned into a political body in essence.

Will Its Politicization Succeed?

Religion transcends politics, but it does not mean that religion cannot show its concern with politics. For example, Buddhism often pray for the emergence of a good monarch—Chakravartin, expecting him to govern the country and benefit people. More than that, Buddhist scriptures even contain some special chapters teaching how to be a good monarch, which deserves to be learned by leaders of all levels in a modern society.

Therefore, the above-mentioned does not mean that Falun Gong shall not turn into a political group, let alone that they shall not criticize politics. But the problem is, in the author's opinion, Li Hongzhi's remarks and behaviors show four obvious political defects, and the political career of his disciples under his leadership probably has a bleak future. Now, the four defects are recounted as follows.

1. Inconsistency

Before the "April 25 Incident", Li Hongzhi repeatedly expressed that he would never participate in politics, and more importantly, he admonished his believers not to have any political remarks and deeds that had nothing to do with practice. For example, he said,

> *"A society of mediocre people, no matter what a kind of society or politics it is, has its destiny; it has been predestined by the Heaven. A person who practices and cultivates himself does not have to care for the matter in such a society that does not concern him, let alone taking part in political struggles."*

> *"Religion and politics cannot be integrated. Once religion involves politics, its leaders will be distracted with secular matters. In this case, he will professedly propagate the pursuit of compassion and the return to the Pure Land, but actually remain evil and hypocritical and pursue fame and interest in his mind. Power is what the people have sought for, and fame is a serious obstacle in the way to consummation. After long, such a person will become the leader of a cult."* ⑩

After the "April 25 Incident", however, Li Hongzhi changed his tune completely! He declared that it was now the "period of true dharma", encouraging his disciples to "eliminate the evil and make clear the truth" by propagating that "The eradication of evils is for the sake of true dharma, not for the cultivation of individuals". (See detail in Section 14, "From Latter Dharma to True Dharma"). How can he conceal such inconsistency and fool the people of insight simply with such deceiving words as "true dharma"?

2. The Display of Incompetence before a Connoisseur

Li Hongzhi and his followers have a strange theory when they criticize the CPC. They look on Jiang Zemin and the CPC differently, and laid all blame on Jiang Zemin as an individual for the 'April 25 Incident', uglifying him to the utmost with bad language. They mention no single word of such present party and political leaders as Hu Jintao, Wen Jiabao, and have never criticized them at all; obviously, they do so intending people to feel that the matter has nothing to do with the CPC. But at the same time, they unexpectedly allege that Jiang Zemin and CPC "utilized each other" and "worked hand in glove" to persecute them, that Jiang persecuted them because he envied and feared them, that the CPC prosecuted them because it has nature as such, and so forth. Such inconsecutive remarks impress people as if they are out of mind. In fact, on the occasion of the "April 25 Incident", Jiang Zemin was the supreme leader both of the CPC and the authorities in the mainland, so Jiang stood for the CPC, and his decision was just that of the CPC, it makes no sense to assert that Jiang and the CPC "utilized each other". When they do so, Li Hongzhi and his followers are obviously imitating the traditional fighting skills of the CPC, which has been good at "looking on issues from the point of view of dialectics", "Everything has its good and bad sides", "isolating the minority and uniting the majority", and "defeating rivals by castigating them to the utmost". The problem is, however, their insane remarks indicate that they are not skillful at such set of skills; so, they are simply displaying their incompetence before a connoisseur when they employ such poor tricks to tackle with the CPC, and the effects are probably very limited.

3. A Wrong Estimate of the Situation

Recently, Li Hongzhi and his followers have frequently alleged in articles in their publications and the internet that the CPC power has been "approaching its doom" already, "its collapse can be expected soon", and so on. Not long ago, the author had a discussion about Kuomintang's policy on its compromise across the Taiwan Straits with some leaders of the Taiwan Falun Dafa Research Society, but they highly disapprove of Kuomintang, and even condemned Ma Ying-jeou for his "surrendering" and so on. They gave such remarks obviously because they had made a wrong estimate of the situation.

Sixteen years ago when Lee Teng-hui was in power, Taiwan adopted the policy of "overcoming impetuosity and exercising patience", which was actually a guideline to "remain detached and expect changes". Consequently, Taiwan missed plenty of opportunity for economic development. Lee Teng-hui chose that policy just because he was convinced by a Japanese scholar, who thought that the CPC was about to collapse, and that the mainland would fall apart. That is the latest lesson of making a wrong estimate of the situation in the mainland. At present, the situation in the mainland is like this: The CPC had adhered to Deng Xiaoping's line of "peaceful development" for more than thirty years, and it has accomplished great achievements in terms of comprehensive national strength; in the foreseeable future, there is no reason to think that it will discontinue such a course, that is, the possibility of "collapse in one day" is very low. The present remarks of Li Hongzhi and his followers are actually a fond dream based on such wrong estimate of the situation, and it cannot come true at all.

4. Arrogance Filling Others with Apprehension

Li Hongzhi regards himself as the only supreme true god in the universe, professing to be superior to the Buddha, Laotze, Confucius and Jesus. His writings are just scriptures; not only that his "disciples" today shall not interpret them, but also that even people thousands of generations later shall not change a single word of them. Such presumptuousness may help draw large groups of slavish followers at a moment if it is used in religion, but for long, it is ineffective after all, for people of insight all know that they cannot leave an arrogant man of such kind free to seize political power, or otherwise it would be a big problem and the people could hardly live on. So, if Li Hongzhi leads his followers to continue in the field of politics, the elite will certainly feel apprehension, they would either flinch or arise to oppose Li and his followers. More seriously, a politician cannot do mere negative things; while he criticizes his rivals, he has to put forwards his own positive political propositions and ideals. Up to the present, however, people have not seen any political views or ideas in Li Hongzhi and his followers, so it will be hard for him to call on the masses in the future.

It is true that Li Hongzhi and his followers have shown enthusiasm for political activities at present, but they certainly cannot go far now that they have contained the above-mentioned four defects. The former two defects belong to the category of political skills, the third one proves their poor political insight, and the fourth one indicates a serious problem of essence; in a word, they are problematic from the most fundamental essence to the most basic skills. Let's illustrate it with a war. In a war, except for successful strategies, clever tactics and strong battle effectiveness, the participants have to comply with the Tao to guarantee their victory (See the *Sunzi on the Art of War*, Chapter 1孫子兵法第一篇). When they are engaged in politics, Li Hongzhi and his organizations are poor in strategies and tactics, especially, they do not comply with the Tao; their only strength lies in their strong battle effectiveness—They have their own propaganda weapons such as newspaper, journal, radio station and website, and they are able to launch street movements all over the world. But what use does it have after all? The author asserts that Li Hongzhi can only play a part of "marginalized political group" no matter how hard his disciples try unless he can accept advice and correct his mistakes.

Notes:
1. See the *New Epoch*, Issue 174, p. 32. A research office of the public security department of the CPC once published an essay titled "Li Hongzhi and His Stories" on July 22, 1999, which is included in the book "*Disclose and Condemn the Heresies of 'Falun Dafa'*". Beijing: Xinhua Publishing House, July 1999, 1st edition. Those who are interested in details can consult it.
2. Before the reform and opening to the outside world in the mainland in 1978, the people were always in short supply of food and clothes. At that

time, those who worked at a unit of grain and oil supply were viewed as an upper class in the eyes of ordinary people.

3. After Chiang Ching-kuo's death on January 13, 1988, Lee Teng-hui gradually seized the power and took the line of Taiwan Independence, and thus caused successive serious conflicts within Kuomintang. Meanwhile, the relations across the Straits entered a stage of delicacy, too; fortunately, thanks to the efforts of several sides, the representatives across the Straits held a peace talk in Singapore at the end of April, 1992. Soon after that, the two sides reached the "1992 consensus" (九二共識) in Hong Kong, which became a foundation for the new prospect of peace across the Straits after Ma Ying-jeou took power in 2008. Before the peace talk in Singapore, related people across the Straits met for several times in Nan Huaijin's residence in Hong Kong at first, and that was actually a prologue of the negotiation in Singapore. Later on, these meetings were described as "Events of Secret Cross-Straits Couriers" (两岸密使事件) in the media. As for the internal conflicts within Kuomintang caused by Lee Teng-hui, see the author's *Personal Witness of Kuomintang's Split in Taiwan* (dictated by Teng Jie), published in the *Biographical Literature*, Issue 502, 2004 (3). With regard to the "Secret Events of Cross-Straits Couriers", see the author's "Refute the Events of Secret Cross-Straits Couriers", in the *Sing Tao Daily*, the page of Cross-Straits Hotline, a newspaper in Hong Kong, May 2-4, 1995.

4. The theory of "*yuan, huei, yuen and shi*" is a philosophy of history of Shao Yong (邵雍alias Shao Kangjie, 1001—1077), a great Neo-

Confucian of the North Dynasty. See details in the *Huang Ji Jing Sh*（皇極經世）*i*.

5. See the note for the essay "Li Hongzhi and His Stories".

6. See the book *"Disclose and Criticize 'Falun Dafa'"*, p. 10. Beijing: Xinhua Publishing House.

7. Li Hongzhi argued overseas that he was merely transferring to another plane in Beijing when the "April 25 Incident" happened. But the CPC authorities invoked an entry and exit record, pointing out that he unexpectedly entered China on April 22 and left Beijing for Hong Kong on the afternoon of April 24 after he gave his followers assignments. Actually, it does not matter who told the truth and who did not. As for the story told by the Chinese authorities, see the essay titled "Li Hongzhi and His Stories" mentioned above, and with respect to that told by Li Hongzhi, see the *Falun Fofa—Essentials for Further Advances* (Vol. Two), p. 15.

8. As for the original text of the CPC official statements quoted below, see the book mentioned in Note 6.

9. The two essays A Few Opinions of Mine published on June 2, 1999 and A Brief Statement of Mine published on July 22 the same year are both included in the book mentioned in Note 7.

10. See the *Falun Fofa—Essentials for Further Advances*, pp. 85 & 91.

The Standards of a Cult

================================

Soon after the "April 25 Incident" in 1999, the Central Government in Beijing defined "Falun Gong" as a "*xiejiao*"(邪教) (cult, literally "evil religion) and banned it all over China. On June 5 the same year, Li Hongzhi, who was in the USA, placed advertisement in important newspapers in Hong Kong, publishing an essay titled "A Few Opinions of Mine" to argue against Beijing. In addition to the exaggeration of "more than one hundred million" disciples, the main points of his arguments are as follows:

> *"Falun Gong has no rules of religion that have to be observed, no temples or churches, and no religious rituals. Practitioners can freely join and abandon the practice as they wish, and there is no list of practitioners. How can it be called a religion? As for the word "evil", Falun Gong teaches people to pursue good, refuse to receive presents and funds, and help people to cure their diseases and improve their physical health. Are such deeds also 'evil'?"* ①

Let's put aside politics. Merely from the point of view of objective principles, Li's arguments as above are untenable. Then, why is that?

What Is Religion?

First, it is doubtless that Li has tried to establish a new religion which respects himself as a hierarch and his "Dafa" as the only doctrine.

The Chinese phrase *"zongjiao"*(宗教) is a translation of "religion" from the West (English, German and French) in the early modern times. Then, what is religion? The definition of "religion" varies in the West, and is very complicated. Usually, it is acknowledged that a religion must contain such elements as a set of "doctrines", a set of "rules" for believers' conduct, and a set of rituals. But meanwhile, there are some looser views, for example, an German religion philosopher Paul Tillich held that anything that contained the essential element of religion, that is, ultimate concern, could be viewed as a "religion". Therefore, a religion does not necessarily have such tangible things as any "lists of practitioners", "temples", "churches" and "rituals". Furthermore, even the hierarchs of a religion can be unfixed, for example, the Brahmanism in ancient India was just different from Buddhism which has Sakyamuni as a hierarch of outstanding personality. Most importantly, it is the basic condition of a religion to have a set of "teachings" (doctrines) on the fundamental and ultimate issues of human life (such as the meaning of life, the destination after death and so on) and encourage people to believe in them. If there is a "hierarch" who serves as a center to propagate such doctrines as well as certain code of conduct (rituals or moral criteria) at the same time, they would constitute the sufficient conditions of a religion.

Now let's estimate "Falun Gong" from the point of view of these features. "Falun Gong" has its "doctrines" constituted with its "Fa" and "Gong", and the part of "Gong" concurrently have the qualities of "rituals" and "criteria". In addition, Li Hongzhi himself has tried hard to play the part of "Master" (actually a hierarch), and has constantly professed that the writings he has propagated are just "scriptures" and prohibited his "disciples" from changing even a single word in them. So, Li's "Falun Gong" has completely had the sufficient conditions of a religion, and he is just deceiving by arguing that his "Falun Gong" is not religion. In fact, Li himself has proclaimed, "Falun Dafa is not a religion, but people in the future will think it a religion." He speaks these words just like a cat that shuts its eyes while stealing creams.

What Is "Evil"?

Secondly, it is relatively complex to make clear the problem of "evil".

In Buddhist scriptures, there are many complex views about whether a religion is "evil" or not, for examples, "non-Buddhist ways based on incorrect causes", "true-thusness with incorrect deeds", "Buddhist sects of wrong opinions", "numerous wrong opinions", "non-Buddhist philosophy which condones the making of one's living by immoral means", "a group whose future follows incorrect paths", "incorrect beliefs", "evil teachings", "three kinds of evils against the right way", "eight kinds of evils against the right way", "evil guidelines", "thorough interpretations made by a contaminated mind" and so on. Here it is not necessary to analyze these terms one by one, but in general, one can judge from three aspects to determine whether a religion is "evil" or not.

Firstly, is it proper in terms of the "teachings" that it embraces?
Secondly, is it proper in terms of the hierarch's "intentions"?
Thirdly, is it proper in terms of the "means" of propaganda?

What needs to be kept in mind is that the above three points vary in sequence in terms of importance. Concretely, we can have following eight sets of combinations:

1. If it is proper in terms of all the three aspects, it is not a cult, of course.
2. If it is improper in terms of all the three aspects, it is a cult, of course.
3. If it is improper in terms of the first aspect but is proper in terms of the 2nd and 3rd aspects, still it is a cult.
4. If it is improper in terms of the 1st and 2nd aspects but is proper in terms of the 3rd aspect, still it is a cult.

5. If it is improper in terms of the 1st and 3rd aspects but is proper in terms of the 2nd aspect, still it is a cult.

6. If it is proper in terms of the 1st aspect but is improper in terms of the other two aspects, it can be conceded not as a cult.

7. If it is proper in terms of the 1st and 2nd aspects but is improper in terms of the 3rd aspect, still it can be conceded not as a cult.

8. If it is proper in terms of the 1st and 3rd aspects but is improper in terms of the 2nd aspect, still it can be conceded not as a cult.

From the point of view of the above combinations, "Falun Gong" can be estimated as following:

In terms of doctrine: In the light of the analysis above, Li Hongzhi's "Fa" (doctrine) is totally a muddle of nouns in Buddhism, Taoism, science and folk supernatural tales that he has collected. Moreover, he has fabricated and twisted the meanings of some plain or basic Buddhist terms (for example, some historical facts in the history of Buddhism, non-duality dharma-gates, three realms, five kinds of supernatural abilities and so forth). Therefore, such a "doctrine" cannot be viewed as proper.

In terms of "intentions": Mencius said, "That whereby the superior man is distinguished from other men is what he preserves in his heart;-- namely, benevolence and propriety."② Both in philosophy and religion in the West and the East, it is the most important to judge a person's intention in making sure whether he is good or evil and right or wrong. Here, the so-called "intentions" just mean "what he preserves in his heart", or "motives". Li Hongzhi calls himself a "master", professing that the "Dafa" that he propagates is at the highest level in the universe, and that he himself is superior to Laotze and the Buddha. And also, he publicly alleges that his writings are "scriptures", forbidding anyone from changing even a single word in them, and expecting to keep it that way for thousands of generations.

All such remarks and behaviors have proven his arrogance and idiocy. Such a character is called "egomania" in modern psychology, and serious "*gong gao wo man*" (貢高我慢self-conceit) in Buddhism. Therefore, it can be affirmed that Li's "intention" does not point at the "superior man" as Mencius mentioned, for he does not have a proper motive in his propaganda of "Dafa".

In terms of "means": A religion should be viewed as a "cult" now that both its "doctrine" and "intention" are improper even if its "means" is uncontroversial. Therefore, Li's excuse that he teaches "people to be good, charge no presents or money, and help people improve their health" is merely at the level of "means"; even if what he says is true, "Falun Gong" is still a cult. That should be beyond question.

Li Hongzhi's Standard

What is funny is that Li Hongzhi himself has mentioned "a standard to identify a cult", and this standard is suitable for him. He says,

"How can some false dharma gates save people? They cannot save people, for what they propagate is not Fa. Of course, some people established certain religions; at first, they did not intend to become devils that destroyed the right religion. They got enlightened somewhat at different levels, and understood a few principles, but they were inferior to those who are truly enlightened, and they were merely at very low levels. They found some principles, finding out that some matters among mediocre people were wrong, and they also told people how to do good deeds. At first, they did not oppose other religions. As a result, people believed them, thinking that what they propagated was reasonable; later on, people increasingly believed them, consequently they began to worship the latter instead of religions. Once they became interested in fame and interests, they wanted the people to worship them as something, and from then on, they established a new religion. I tell you, people, all

these are cults; even if they do not intend to do harms to the people, they are still cults, for they prevent the people from believing in right religions: right religions have been intended for saving people, but a cult cannot. After long, they would do bad things stealthily. Recently, many of such cults have been introduced into China, for example, the so-called Guanyin Famen（觀音法門） is just one of them. So, you people do take care, for it is said that there are more than 2,000 kinds of cults in a certain country in East Asia; in Southeast Asia and Western countries, there are various beliefs, and in a certain country, there is even a religion of witchery."③

They "told people how to do good deeds", does Li Hongzhi not teach people to do good deeds likewise, boasting to "charge no fees, cure diseases and improve physical health"?

"Once they became interested in fame and interests, they wanted the people to worship them as something, and from then on, they established a new religion." In comparison, however, Li Hongzhi calls himself a "master", and he is the only one qualified as a "master". His speeches are just scriptures…Is it not a self-portrait of himself?

"Consequently they began to worship the latter instead of religions." Li Hongzhi attracts people with Buddhist terms at first, after they are drawn to his side, he professes that his "Dafa" is not a thing of Buddhism; instead, it is superior to that of Sakyamuni. Is he not publicly telling people to believe in his "Hongchuan Dafa"（洪傳大法） only instead of Buddhism?

"All these are cults; even if they do not intend to do harms to the people, they are still cult." This remark Li Hongzhi has made marvelously! It does not seem to be unfair at all that Beijing defined "Falun Gong" as a "cult", for it exactly meets the standard that Li himself has established.

Notes:

1. An advertisement on the *Ming Pao*（香港：明報），
   June 5, 1999, p. A14. And also, this essay has
   been included into the *Essentials for Further
   Advances* (Vol. Two).
2. *The Writings of Mencius*, Liu Lou (Part Two)
3. *Zhuan Falun*, p. 111.

Postscript for the English Version

In March and April last year, the Chinese version of this book was respectively published in Hong Kong and Taiwan, and rapidly drew the attention of Chinese-speaking readers all over the world, and related reports in the internet amount up to more than 400,000 items. Li Hongzhi and his organization must have felt the impact of this book, hence they let out various messages about their possible "counterattack".

Actually, it is not necessary to "counterattack" this book; instead, it could produce only contrary effects if anyone did so. This book starts with a cultural worker's curiosity and his attempt to maintain the orthodox faith in Buddhist doctrines, without any other backgrounds or motives. In addition, the whole book is completely rational discussion and question about Li's "Dafa" theory, and contains no smearing or attacking words. It could only make the truth clearer if one wants to "counterattack" such a book. Therefore, I publicly claimed in several newspapers in Taiwan last year that any people who dissent from this book are welcome to point out the author's defects or debate with the author.

With an overall view of all he remarks and practical actions of Li in the two decades since his establishment of <Falun Gong>, his true objective is to establish a new religion that respects himself as a hierarch and "surmounts all the other religions forever". Li has constantly claimed that both Sakyamuni in Buddhism and Laozi in Taoism were inferior to him, and that even the Jehovah, St. Mary and Jesus Christ in Christianity were merely ordinary "gods" or "goddess" at a lower level of the "universe Buddhist Dharma", who were thus neither the Savior nor the Creator. As for Brahmanism in India, Li even classifies it as an evil "cult". Li has even alleged that only what he has preached is "the highest Buddhist Dharma of the universe", and that it is great teaching that has never been heard in the past and will never be seen in the future. People have to believe in "Master Li" if they want to be redeemed. In a word, <Falun Gong> has not only destroyed the orthodox faith in Buddhism and Taoism, but also undermined the orthodox faith in Christianity (including Catholicism, Protestantism and Orthodox Church) and other religions in the world. And because of this, I decide to publish the English version of this book one year later after the publication of its Chinese one, so that people all over the world, especially English-speaking readers, have a chance to learn deeply about Li's "Dafa", and thus maintain the orthodox faith in Christianity and other religions.

It is a heavy task to put the Chinese version of this book into English, for it involves many abstruse concepts and special nouns both in religion and philosophy in the West and the East. I do not know English well enough to do this work at all; luckily I found the help from several friends from Hong Kong and Taiwan, spent more than one year to complete the translation. Particularly, I would like to thank Mr. Xu Chengzong the general editor of the Hong Kong Times and Mr. Kuo QiChuang from the USA, who have made most attributions to it.

Lao Chengwu
May 2012
Vimalakīrti Cultural Center, Yangmei, Taiwan